may be kept

Burglarproof

A Complete Guide to Home Security

James Edward Keogh
John Koster

McGraw-Hill Book Company

New York   St. Louis   San Francisco   Auckland   Bogotá
Düsseldorf   Johannesburg   London   Madrid
Mexico   Montreal   New Delhi   Panama
Paris   São Paulo   Singapore
Sydney   Tokyo   Toronto

Library of Congress Cataloging in Publication Data

Keogh, James, date.
  Burglarproof.

  Includes index.
  1. Burglary protection. I. Koster, John, date, joint author. II. Title.
TH9705.K46   643   76-48090
ISBN 0-07-034146-X

1234567890   MUBP   786543210987

*The editors for this book were Robert A. Rosenbaum and Gretlyn Blau, the de-
signer was Naomi Auerbach, and the production supervisor was Frank P. Bel-
lantoni. It was set in Palatino by J. C. Meyer & Son, Inc.*

Printed by The Murray Printing Company and bound by The Book Press.

Contents

Preface

Let's face facts. You can expect to have your home burglarized twice in your lifetime. This statement is based on randomized statistics of present crime figures.

Obviously, two burglaries in a lifetime are two more than anyone should have to put up with, but that's not the worst part of the story. Crime figures have been on a drastic increase since the 1960s and show no signs of leveling off. From 1960 to 1970, the last census year, the population increased 13 percent while the crime rate increased 144 percent. Since 1970, population growth has slowed down, but the crime rate has continued to increase. By 1980, you may expect your home to be burglarized three times, four times, or even more often.

Burglary, like lightning, all too often strikes more than twice. Some people who live in inner cities, or even in some suburbs, wouldn't find two burglaries *a year* to be out of the ordinary. And those who can least afford to be plundered, the wage-earners who have a hard time replacing their few luxury items or senior citizens on fixed incomes, are the most frequent victims.

Burglary, like all other crime, is spiraling. The real reason for the increase in burglary is that it's an easy way to make a good living if you aren't afraid to run a few risks and work unusual hours. Through their innocence or ignorance, or through apathy, most home-owners or apartment dwellers make it so easy for a burglar to rip them off that he'd have to be crazy to consider honest work. If some fascist state of the future revived public torture and garroting for anyone caught stealing a radio or tape recorder, thieves would still practice their arts if they knew their chances of being caught were far less awesome than the chance of meeting violent death on the nation's highways. Better police work and stricter laws are important, but constant harping on these expensive placebos by politicians only takes the stress away from where it belongs—on the property-owner himself. He can do more to protect his home than any law enforcement agency or court.

Make no mistake about it, to be burglarized is an unpleasant experience. Besides losing large amounts of private property—and believe it or not, replacing the losses of disposable valuables from even a middle-income home can run into thousands of dollars—there is a profound sense of shock attached to coming home and finding your living room and bedrooms torn apart and your treasured possessions carted off to no-one-knows-where, or broken and scattered all over the floor. For many people, a burglary can cause a worse emotional trauma than a serious car crash or the death of a relative. There is also the unpleasant but distinct possibility that you may surprise a burglar in the process of robbing your home. In most cases, nothing will happen, but some burglars—particularly the younger, crazier ones in slum areas, who have no respect for any human or legal sanction—make it a practice to kill anyone who comes upon them in the act. Savage beatings and rape, though not common, are also quite possible.

All in all, it's worth a lot of time and energy, and some expense, to avoid being burglarized. This book will tell you what the best methods are to do this.

The authors make no claims for infallibility. The kind of professional thief who does things like digging tunnels from sewer systems into bank vaults isn't going to be foiled by the methods we advocate. But the amateur burglar, who is both the most frequent and the most dangerous violator of people's homes and apartments, can be dissuaded from picking your place nine times out of ten if you follow the methods we describe in simple detail. This is not a book for technological experts, criminologists, or lovers of detective fiction. It's a brass-tacks manual to prevent YOU from being the victim of burglary and its possible tragic consequences.

James Edward Keogh
John Koster

1

How Burglaries Are Committed

PROFILE OF A THIEF

It has long been a maxim among military men that the road to victory begins with knowing your enemy. Thus the homeowner or apartment dweller who wishes to avoid being burglarized should have at least a beginner's knowledge of the thief and how he operates.

Over the last ten or fifteen years, a rash of "caper" films have romanticized certain highly skilled thieves, men who will stop at nothing to plunder expensive prizes. The scenario may include the thief lowering himself spiderlike down the sides of buildings with ropes, digging tunnels from adjoining buildings into bank vaults, or using elaborate disguises to ingratiate himself with the prospective victim.

Such thieves exist, but unless you, as a homeowner, happen to be harboring the Hope Diamond or the Star of India in your split-level or efficiency apartment, the odds on running into one are almost nil.

There are, however, professional thieves who sometimes steal from the average homeowner, particularly from the more well-to-do homeowner. These professionals account for a relatively small percentage of burglaries and larcenies, but they are worth examining both for their own sake and for the sake of contrast to the much more common amateur thief, who is the real threat to the ordinary homeowner.

Professional thieves exist in a world of their own. They often travel around the country in troupes, almost always by car, they dress conservatively, and they stay at good but inconspicuous hotels and other lodgings. They have words and expressions unique to their trade, and many of these expressions have been around for hundreds of years. The professional thief usually keeps a large amount of money ready to hand, either leaving it with a trusted associate or carrying it on his person. This is known as "fall money," and is used either to bribe arresting officials or to post bond if and when the professional is arrested. The professional also has access to good lawyers and bondsmen, and is quite often able to extricate himself from some very bad situations through a combination of fast talking, bribery, and legal chicanery. Most professional thieves eventually spend some time in jail, but they regard this as a professional risk, much as a ski instructor takes broken bones in his stride or a high-iron worker accepts the risk of fatal falls from tall buildings.

When professional thieves are in action, they dress as inconspicuously as possible. Thus in burglarizing homes in a middle-class neighborhood, they would wear suits or casual suburban togs. To steal from a warehouse, they might dress as truck drivers.

The professional, unlike the amateur, doesn't go around haphazardly breaking into any house that looks unoccupied at the moment. Professionals, working alone or, more often, in teams, use all available sources of information and often study their victims for weeks or months before they make a move. Invariably, they pick high-priced items, such as valuable goods in a warehouse or jewels and artwork of known value in a wealthy individual's home. Some of them steal on contract from "respectable" citizens.

Theft by contract is not common, but it happens often enough to be worth mentioning. A New Jersey doctor and his

The professional burglar carries special tools, like this lockpicking device, demonstrated by a police detective. (Courtesy of Ed Hill.)

wife were victims of a contract burglary inspired and arranged by "friends" of the family. The doctor and his wife were at a party where his wife showed off some expensive and rare jewelry that she set great store by. Unfortunately for her, one of the guests also took a fancy to the rare jewelry and decided that he (or she) must have it at all costs. Since the items were one of a kind and since the doctor's wife was a collector, purchase was out of the question. There was no legal way of obtaining the jewelry.

The would-be owner made a few contacts with shady characters—which is less difficult than the average person thinks. An agreement was reached with a professional thief, who agreed to break into the doctor's house and steal the desired jewelry for 20 percent of the retail value of the jewels. This was on the low side for a professional job; 50 percent would have been more usual. For some reason, however, the thief agreed to the 20 percent deal. Perhaps he realized that disposing of such rare jewels to a "fence" (receiver of stolen goods) would be next to impossible and thought 20 percent was the best he could do.

Within a month of the party where the would-be owner had first seen the jewels, the professional thief entered the doctor's home and stole the jewels and nothing more. The doctor called the police, reported the incident, and collected his insurance, and the doctor's wife never saw her jewels again.

There are two lessons to be learned from this incident. The first is that making an ostentatious display of rare or expensive jewelry is unwise. The second is that having once purchased expensive jewelry, the owners shouldn't assume that they can protect their treasures merely be locking a door behind them when they go out. Generally, any item of great value should be stored with a competent guard service or in a bank's safety deposit vault until it is to be worn.

Most of us, however, are not in the doctor's class and have little to fear from the professional burglar, whose target is expensive jewelry. The greatest threat to the average homeowner or apartment dweller's property—and his life—is the amateur burglar, who steals indiscriminately, often to support a drug habit, or sometimes because he is unable or unwilling to take up another mode of work. This sort of thief doesn't select his victim solely from the high-income bracket or the social register.

Unlike the professional thief, the amateur rarely takes the trouble to dress to blend with his surroundings. He may wear work clothes or perhaps the tacky finery associated with the drug culture. Unlike the armed robber, who may pull a stocking over his face, the burglar almost never wears a mask and doesn't otherwise emulate the cartoon crooks of an old Dick Tracy comic strip or a Batman comic book.

The amateur burglar doesn't usually plan his jobs in advance. He most often breaks into a house or apartment, rips off everything in sight, making a mess in the process, and then tries to sell the items as best he can. Those with a vague sheen of professionalism usually work with a fence, who may be anything from a pawnbroker (though many pawnbrokers are reputable and honest) to the owner of a tavern or bar. There are bars in almost every major city where people in the

A potential burglar loiters on a suburban street. Don't hesitate to notify police about loiterers on foot or in parked cars. (Courtesy of Mike SanGiovanni.)

know "shop" for color TVs or stereo sets, no questions asked, at a fraction of their retail price.

Those thieves who have no access to a fence or who believe they can do better on their own try to sell the stolen goods on their own. Some of them conduct rummage sales out of the trunks of cars. Others approach merchants or other potential customers surreptitiously and offer them bargains that are difficult to refuse. There have been cases of warehouse thievery where a retailer's rivals had clothing the retailer had ordered on their racks before the retailer did. Thieves had stolen the goods in transit and sold them to the retailer's competitors.

Many amateur thieves are drug addicts who desperately need money to feed their habits. A heroin habit can run the addict hundreds of dollars per week just for drugs, and heroin users are consequently among the most avaricious of all thieves. Some of them will steal from houses even when the owners are at home, simply by rushing into the building, grabbing the first valuable article they see, and fleeing before the startled homeowner can react. Amateur thieves, especially those on drugs, are often armed and always dangerous. Unlike the professional thief, who knows the ins and outs of the prison systems and probably has ready access to lawyers and bondsmen, the amateur dreads being arrested and confined, because he has no money for a lawyer or bondsman and because he will probably have to kick his drug habit "cold turkey"—without any drug aids. This is an agonizing process that may involve days of torment.

For this reason, the amateur burglar, clumsy as he is, is much more dangerous than the professional. The professional rarely carriers a gun and uses it even more rarely. If he is surprised in the act of burglary, he will usually withdraw as quickly as possible or if cornered, will try to talk his way out of trouble. The amateur burglar, on the other hand, is apt to panic and start shooting or slashing his way out of a jam. Thus care should be taken to avoid a direct confrontation with any burglar, amateur or professional. It may seem quite natural for the indignant homeowner to rush upon anyone who dares to enter his castle and to demand an explanation. It may also be fatal.

The amateur burglar is thus both the most dangerous and the most common, and the one of most concern to the average homeowner, who stands to lose a good deal from a break-in, even if he doesn't own any large diamonds or original Rembrandts.

The amateur will enter a home either by day or by night. This sounds simplistic, but the two types of theft are very different and should be discussed at some length.

The main difference is the manner in which the thief selects his targets. Here is a story to illustrate why this is important:

In a suburb of Los Angeles, a couple thought they had made adequate security preparations by buying and installing a light timer for their house lights. The timer, set in advance, switched the light in their living room on at a prearranged time. Any thief, the couple assumed, would be scared away by a light in the window, especially since the light could be seen snapping on and off. With their minds at peace, they loaded up the car and took off for a weekend vacation.

A burglar, however, was working the neighborhood and noticed that about 6 P.M. the light in the living room switched on in the otherwise quiet house. The burglar made a mental note of this, though the first night he confined his attentions to a house up the street from the one with the timer.

The following night, at exactly the same time, the timer snapped the light on again. The burglar knew that most people adhere to some sort of schedule, but he also knew that few people do everything at precisely the same time every night. The precise schedule and the general unoccupied appearance of the house gave him more than a hint that nobody was home.

The burglar decided to give it a try. He walked up to the door and rang the bell. After keeping his finger on the bell for a full minute without results, he pounded the door with his fist. When no one answered, his suspicion seemed confirmed. Using a credit card, the burglar pried open the lock and entered the house. Chalk up one more statistic for suburban L.A. When the couple arrived home late Sunday night, they couldn't believe their eyes. After all, they had taken precautions. The light was on.

The burglar in this case, though hardly a professional, was hip enough to realize that light timers were a tried and tired precaution against burglary, and bold enough to investigate when be became suspicious. When the other signs around the house didn't add up to a family at home, he broke in. The couple's precaution had given the burglar a day's pause and staved off his break-in that long. Most homeowners virtually invite burglars to break into their houses through a total lack of security.

The *night burglar*, like the one in this story, usually drives up and down blocks looking for houses to break into, meaning, most often, those that are poorly lit. Any house that doesn't have some lights showing between 7 and 11 P.M. is an obvious target for a burglary. One of the best lights to leave on when the homeowner is absent is the bathroom light. Even if left on all night, this won't usually strike the burglar as suspicious, and may persuade him that someone is up late "burning the midnight oil."

Another thing burglars look for is homes that are poorly lit on the outside. If a house is completely dark on the outside, or screened from view of the street by trees and bushes, the burglar can hide outside the house to investigate or break in more or less at leisure. Few people realize that turning on a light to scare away a burglar also applies to lights that illuminate the porch or front door of the front yard.

One clear clue for burglars that the house in question is empty is when they see the lights turned on but no car parked in the garage or next to the house. A lighted home with no car equals an empty home, as far as the burglar is concerned.

Once having picked a likely house, the night thief will approach the house on foot and boldly ring the doorbell, like any casual caller. If anyone answers, the thief will simply claim to be lost and go back to his car to select another house.

The night thief usually avoids corner houses at night because houses built on a corner are usually well lit and it is too easy for a thief to be surprised by passing cars—especially passing police cars. The discerning burglar prefers to pass them up for houses where he can watch the road from both sides as he pries the lock open. With many houses to choose from, the burglar will tend to pass up homes that are well lit inside and out, just as he will usually avoid homes with barking dogs inside or nearby. He may also avoid a house where a radio is playing inside or where there is a similar sign that someone is home.

The *day burglar* is somewhat different from the night burglar, and his methods are a bit more sophisticated. The day burglar obviously can't patrol by day and seek out targets by checking on the lights in various houses. He has recourse to completely different tactics.

A story illustrates the tactics of the semipro daytime burglar:

Some time ago, a woman who lived in the state of Washington traveled to New York City. She had spent months planning her trip to the Big Apple. Unfortunately, she didn't spend much time planning to protect her apartment from unwanted visitors while she was away.

The apartment she lived in was three stories tall and had a

Houses in the middle of the block are preferable to corner houses for most thieves. (Courtesy of Mike SanGiovanni.)

A corner house offers a special challenge to the thief, since police patrols may come from either direction. But too much shrubbery obscures the view. (Courtesy of Mike SanGiovanni.)

so-called open-door policy. Anyone who wanted to could enter the building and go to any apartment he wanted to without interference. Some residents liked this because they didn't have to worry about opening the door while burdened with two armloads of groceries. Unfortunately, the friendly neighborhood burglar liked the open-door policy too. On his tour of the unprotected building, the burglar discovered that the woman's apartment was vacant, broke in, and made off with all the valuables he could find, tearing the apartment apart and breaking a good deal of the contents in the process.

The Washington woman had made the most obvious mistake that a homeowner or apartment dweller can make when leaving on a long trip: she had forgotten to notify the post office to hold her mail for her, and by the second day of her trip, letters and junk mail had already begun to clutter her mailbox. To compound the mistake, she had also forgotten to notify the local paper to stop its home delivery until she returned. Papers piled in front of her door and the jam-packed mailbox made it obvious that she wasn't at home. She paid heavily for her naïveté, not only in material damages but in the shock and frustration of finding her apartment torn apart as if a typhoon had blown through it.

Her mistakes were glaringly obvious and a virtual invitation to plunder. But daylight burglars have ways of gathering information that don't always depend on such blatant carelessness. Many semipro burglars make daily trips to supermarkets and other places which offer public bulletin boards. Here people post notices of items for sale. The thief also consults the classified advertisements in the local papers and the death and wedding notices. Just as the salesman may pick up leads from these sources to tell him where he can make a sale, the thief uses them to find targets. For instance, the enterprising burglar who knows that a bereaved family will be gathered for a funeral or a joyous family will be convened for a wedding can have the whole day to plunder their home with virtual impunity while the mourners or revelers are busy elsewhere.

Similarly, the thief who knows from ads in local papers that a family is trying to sell some article of value may decide to relieve them of it free of charge. Since these ads usually provide the reader with the would-be seller's phone number, they constitute all the information a thief needs.

Most people who place an ad of an item for sale want interested individuals to call within certain hours. This is often because they are not at home during other hours. Thus if a thief notices that the instruction is given to call between 7 and 10 P.M., the thief assumes that the person who placed the ad is out at work and not at home. So the thief makes a phone call to the home that placed the ad from a pay phone booth in the vicinity. When the phone begins to ring, the thief listens for a few moments, and if no one answers, he lets the phone dangle and go on ringing while he rushes with all proper haste to the target home or apartment. If the phone is still ringing when he arrives outside the door, he can assume that no one is home. If, on the other hand, the phone is silent, someone may have finally picked it up and the thief is hesitant.

Assuming that the phone is still ringing, the thief may then ring the doorbell and let it ring for a solid minute or so. He may also pound on the door before breaking in, by using his credit card or burglar tools to pry open the lock or sometimes just by kicking the door down. He removes the article advertised, rifles through the house for any other valuables, and then departs.

Unlike the night thief, the day thief doesn't object to houses on the corner since there is one less neighbor to worry about. And, if someone should chance to answer the door, the day thief, like the night thief, excuses himself as a lost wayfarer, a salesman, or some such dodge, and departs as quickly as possible without arousing suspicion.

Most day thieves are after profit, plain and simple, and try to avoid contact with the homeowner as much as possible. Unfortunately, there are exceptions. A father-and-son burglar team recently spread a wave of terror across communities from Baltimore to northern New Jersey by their rampage of daylight burglaries which sometimes lapsed into forcible sex acts and ultimately ended in murder.

The father, allegedly a Philadelphia shoemaker, used his eleven-year-old son to find out if anyone was at home. The boy canvassed areas of various affluent suburbs, always near bus lines—incredibly, they traveled by bus. Where no one answered the doorbell, the boy returned with his father and the homes were burglarized. In several cases, however, when attractive women answered the door, they were forced inside the house and ordered to strip and sometimes to perform sex acts. Finally, in New Jersey, a pretty young nurse was murdered by the father when she allegedly refused to perform a sex act. The father-and-son burglary team fled in a panic but were apprehended because of a stupid error. The father discarded a bloody shirt without bothering to destroy the laundry mark on the collar, and the FBI and local police were able to locate the cleaner who had last laundered the shirt and through him, to apprehend the thieves.

Most day thieves never become enmeshed in kinky forced sex acts and in murder, but otherwise the tactics of the father and son were those of the standard daylight burglar. Some daylight burglaries do end in rape and, more rarely, in murder, but this is usually because a woman blunders in on the thieves by accident, and not because of any premeditation. Usually the homeowner is the very last thing the burglar wants to encounter.

APARTMENT BURGLARIES

To the untrained observer, it would seem that a burglar would encounter greater difficulties in stealing from an apartment house than he would in plundering a suburban home. But this is not always the case. In some cases, the burglar may have an easier time cleaning out an apartment than he would breaking into a private home.

The burglar's chief problem in stealing from an apartment house is access. In the case of the woman from Washington, where the apartment building had an open-door policy, this proved to be no problem at all. The burglar simply entered the apartment as if he lived there and unobtrusively looked over the mailboxes as he walked the halls. Those apartments which have mailboxes in a central location near the front door provide a virtual registry of who is out. The thief merely has to find the name and apartment number of anyone whose mail-box is filled to overflowing (whether with letters or with junk mail labeled "Occupant" makes no difference). When he finds a likely target, the burglar makes his way to the apartment and after ringing and knocking, uses his trusty credit card or strip of celluloid to pry open the slip bolt lock and enter. The experienced thief never enters without knocking, though not out of any vestigial remnant of courtly manners.

If the apartment house doesn't have an open-door policy, the thief's life is complicated, but he can still get inside, one way or another. One method involves ostentatious good manners. If each resident has his own key, the thief may loiter at the street entrance and hold the door for a person who has a key. Then, with the keyholder safely inside, the thief himself enters and looks for a likely target. This is a bit risky, since a person who sees the thief do this, or encounters him in the lobby and realizes that he doesn't belong there, may call the police. When they arrive, the thief who doesn't have a good excuse ready may be arrested as a disorderly person or for failure to give a good account of himself, depending on what city or state the apartment is situated in. On the other hand, if the thief has any inkling that the police are on their way, he can usually slip out.

There are other ways to penetrate an apartment complex. Some apartment buildings have delivery entrances with an open-door policy in effect. Instead of using the main lobby and interfering with the tenants, the delivery boy will be encouraged to use the back entrance. So the thief pretends to be a delivery boy and gets into the building with ease.

Some of the better apartments employ a doorman to provide services and protection for their patrons. The doorman, who may or may not be in uniform, stands at the main entrance greeting everyone who enters or leaves. He knows most of them by their faces and names. But because doormen's jobs are usually low paid and often go to senior citizens, there is a rapid turnover, and many doormen don't get a chance to learn the name and face of everyone who lives in a large building.

Thus a thief who dresses like the regular residents of the apartment and proceeds through the entrance as if he be-

longed there has an excellent chance of getting past the doorman. The doorman may not know everyone in the apartment
building, or he may not be able to place the thief but will
assume that his memory has failed and may wish to avoid
embarrassment. Like all too many other people in our modern
society, the doorman may choose to neglect the letter of his
duty to avoid getting in trouble with the boss. So the thief is
able to enter the building despite the doorman.

Once inside, the thief can roam the halls almost at will,
dressed, as he is, like most of the other residents. Since few
apartment dwellers know their neighbors even by name, few
if any residents will realize that he doesn't belong there. Even
those who know their neighbors may assume that he is merely
a new resident. The thief counts on this logic to protect him.
The thief who is plundering a large apartment building will
generally prefer to break into units on the first two or three
floors unless he has a specific reason to do otherwise. The
lower floors shorten the distance that he has to run if he needs
to make a quick getaway in case the unit owner returns home
and discovers him at work. Any apartment on a higher floor
increases the distance that the thief has to run and ups the
odds that he'll be caught on the way down.

Just as the thief prefers to break into houses with the front
door blocked from view on the street, the thief who's working
apartments will prefer to enter an apartment at the end of a
hall, where the lighting is poor. Here he can go to work on the
door in semidarkness and with no fear of passing residents
asking him what he's doing.

A really determined thief may decide to use a disguise to
enter an apartment. He may dress as a painter, or—a favorite
disguise—as a locksmith. Other favorites include disguises as
furniture movers, which allows burglars to carry art objects
and expensive furniture out of an apartment with the same
impunity that real-life furniture movers enjoy when they
move the furniture *in*. One young couple, about to be married,
spent most of their savings on luxurious furniture for their
apartment, only to find out that, a few days before the wedding, thieves had entered the uninhabited apartment dis-

guised as furniture movers and carried off everything but the kitchen sink. This put quite a damper on their wedding.

More crude thieves sometimes resort to climbing the fire escapes to get into apartments when the doors are all locked or guarded. This is pretty obvious, and the smart thief, if he uses this method at all, will only climb a few floors off the ground for fear of being detected and caught. The smarter thieves tend to leave fire escapes alone. There are many better ways to get into a locked apartment.

HOW BURGLARS GET KEYS

The thief of any experience whatever can usually open a *slip bolt lock*, which is the most common type, with a credit card or some other strip of celluloid. He simply slips the plastic card between the door and the door frame near the lock and works the bolt back into the lock. Thus a slip bolt lock is almost useless against a thief of any skill or experience.

If the apartment is equipped with a *dead bolt lock*, the thief has problems. A dead bolt lock, in which the owner must turn the key to close the bolt, cannot be picked with a credit card or other simple device. The really expert thief may pick the lock with special tools—or perhaps with a tool as simple as a hairpin—but lockpicking is an advanced skill, and most amateur thieves don't know how to pick a lock properly. The typical thief will pass up a house which has a dead bolt lock as not worth the trouble and risk, and go on to find easier pickings—or no "picking" at all, as with a slip bolt lock.

But the thief has another option open. If he really wants to get inside, he may be able to obtain a key.

Obtaining a key sounds like something out of a spy movie or one of those high-class caper films. In fact, it may be easier than the homeowner realizes to get a key, and may not entail mugging, seduction, or any of the other methods so dear to the hearts of movie and TV writers and detective story fans.

Physical attack, let alone seduction, would probably be the last thing on the thief's mind when it comes to obtaining keys. One of the most basic but most fruitful ways to find a house key is to search the outside of the building in question in the vicinity of the front door.

Many people, having been locked out of their house at least once, take care to leave a key near the door where they can find it in case they lose the key they carry on their person or in their car. They invariably seem to think that the spots they pick to hide these keys are furtive and clever, but the experienced thief probably knows all of them backward and forward.

The most common places are: inside mailboxes, under a door mat, over the door on the lintel, on a windowsill, or in the dirt of a convenient flowerpot. These spots are very handy for the homeowner who has left his pocket key at home. Unfortunately, they are equally handy for the thief. A quick search of all the usual hiding places will only take him a few moments.

There are other ways to get keys. If an apartment dweller moves into a new unit and doesn't bother to change the lock, the apartment landlord, the superintendent, the previous tenants, the handyman, and the immediate families of the previous tenants will all probably have keys. This multiplies the odds on the keys falling—or being placed—in the wrong hands.

Of course, it would be paranoid to assert that each and every one of these people is a potential burglar. But even if every one of them were scrupulously honest, they could easily lose the keys or have them stolen. And it is not out of the question that one or more of the people who have spare keys would either use them to break in on their own or sell them to thieves. There is a thriving traffic in hotel and motel room keys among thieves who bribe maids or clerks in the manager's office. Thieves who work hotels or motels are always eager to get their hands on keys, which facilitate a quiet entry, and they can often find one or more dissatisfied employees willing to sell keys for a small consideration or a share in the loot.

Homeowners aren't immune. They have the same problem where keys are concerned as those who live in apartments or travel to hotels and motels. If the homeowner doesn't change the locks on her door when she moves into a new house, she must expect that the previous owner, the real estate agent, and the agent's employees, among others, all have keys. Friends of the former owner may also have keys. The possibilities are literally endless. Again, it is possible that every one of these keyholders is absolutely honest. But consider the odds.

A true story illustrates the problems inherent in letting keys get out of the homeowner's possession:

A while ago, in Georgia, a single man placed his modest house up for sale. Since he had a friend in the real estate business, he let this friend handle the entire transaction, and gave him a key to the house. He was confident that his friend wouldn't steal anything. After all, he had known him for years.

A few days after the house went up for sale, a young couple arrived at the real estate man's office and asked if they could see the house. The agent, who was glad at the chance of a quick sale, removed the key from a board on his office wall and took the young couple on a tour of the house. The couple seemed interested—very interested, in fact—but made no firm commitment to buy.

Back at the office, the real estate man placed the key back on the board on his wall. As they were preparing to leave the office, the young woman distracted the agent for a moment while her "husband" furtively removed the key from the wallboard and pocketed it. The couple left the agent's office, had a duplicate key made, and then returned to the office and said they wanted to talk about the situation at greater length. While the husband conversed with the agent, who was busily trying to make a sale, the wife tried to replace the key on the wall. But she was unable to do so and secretively dropped the key on the floor instead.

When the agent found the key lying on the floor the next day, he assumed that he had dropped it himself and replaced it on the wall, safe and sound. He soon forgot the young couple who had toured the house.

The young couple, however, forgot nothing. They waited until a new family had purchased the house and moved in, then brought their copy of the key out of retirement and paid the new owners a surprise visit while they were away. Chalk up another statistic.

Even if a new lock were installed in every house, there

would still be plenty of spare keys floating around in the hands of locksmiths and their employees. Again, most locksmiths are honest, but some, of course, are not, just as not all policemen or schoolteachers or bankers are pillars of upright civic virtue. Changing the locks is clearly a must for a good home security, but if a professional thief really wants your key, he can probably get it. And it won't involve hitting you over the head to do it.

INSIDE INFORMATION

We live in the age of the "information explosion," where the purveying of information through books, newspapers, TV, movies, and computer-retrieval systems has come almost to equal agriculture and manufacturing as a major national industry. But one of the oldest professions in the world—thievery—has long had access to information systems that don't depend on cathode tubes or computer memory banks. The thief's usual source of information is by word of mouth—sometimes by overhearing inadvertent conversations and sometimes by paying tipsters to set up victims for him.

A true story illustrates how the thief's information service works:

In New England, some time ago, a middle-aged couple moved into what they believed was a completely secure apartment building. A doorman, on duty twenty-four hours a day, carefully checked everyone who entered the building. At the delivery entrance, a guard not only took the license number of every car that entered the delivery entrance lot, but carefully checked the driver's personal identification and called up the apartment residents who were supposedly receiving the package to make sure that they were really expecting a delivery. The security system seemed to be worthy of Fort Knox. There was even a guard who patrolled the halls every hour on the hour to look for intruders, and between patrols he kept an eye on the garage. Needless to say, the middle-aged couple felt quite secure inside this veritable fortress.

Several months after the couple had moved in, a thief paid them an unwanted visit, and they returned home one night to find everything of value stripped from their luxury apartment, and the apartment itself a shambles. The only thing they could do was to call the police and their insurance company. Police and residents alike were puzzled by the break-in because there were no marks of forcible entry and because the building, which seemed as strong and stalwart as Gibraltar, had been burglarized previously less than two months before.

As time went by, the burglaries at the security fortress continued, always without a trace of forcible entry. It took the police almost a year to catch the thief, who was surprised while rummaging through an apartment, and to find out how the mystifying thefts had been committed. The key to the thefts was inside information.

Personnel was the Achilles' heel of the security fortress apartment building. Both the doorman at the front entrance and the guard at the delivery entrance had been "moonlighting" in addition to their regular jobs by selling information to local crooks. Both the doorman and the delivery entrance guard knew when someone in the building was out, and for emergency purposes, both of them were equipped with keys to every apartment in the building. These, of course, were issued with the purpose of enabling the doorman and the guard to rush to the aid of anyone who was sick or injured or otherwise in need of help. But this charitable purpose backfired when the doorman and guard had several sets of keys made up for their own commercial purposes.

Whenever a thief known to the doorman or the guard approached for a little inside help on a job, the doorman or guard would drop the key on the ground and turn his back. The supposed protectors of the apartment house routinely received $25 to $40 for this consideration. Sometimes, when the doorman or guard staked out a resident's apartment and told the burglars when the resident was out, they demanded, and received, a 10 percent kickback for their inside information. This rather extreme example of inside information cost the residents of the apartment building thousands of dollars in property loss, not to mention the shock of coming home to find their most valuable possessions stolen and their apartments torn apart.

Not all inside information which leads to burglaries is gained through direct collusion between crooks and dishonest security personnel. Some of it may come from the victim's own friends and relatives or the victim himself. Take as an example the person leaving for his vacation. How many people will he inform that he'll be out of town? The homeowner may mention, while chatting at a store counter with a close friend, that he'll be away for a week or a month, only to be overheard by someone else waiting at the counter. In a small town, this mere statement may be enough, since the thief may know the man's name and where he lives, or he may ask the storekeeper unobtrusively, "Is that Mrs. Jones's boy, Roger?"

"No," the storekeeper will answer, innocently enough, "That's Charlie Smith." The thief now has his name, and may be able to get his address with equal ease. Should this fail, there are other methods.

The thief's next step may be to take down the man's license number and then go to a nearby police station, where he isn't known to be a thief and may even be considered a trusted citizen. Here he can tell the police that the man's car scraped against his own but the man drove away before he could complain to him about it. He wants the name so that he can get in touch and settle the matter like a gentleman, out of court. If the police run a computerized license number check on the thief's behalf, he will have not only the man's name but also his address in a matter of seconds.

Consider the endless possibilities: As many as a dozen people may know when you leave for vacation—the newsboy, the mailman, the milkman, your neighbors, the gas station attendant, possibly travel agents, airline personnel, and the staff at any hotels or motels you may stay in. Most of these people are probably honest. Some of them probably are not. Even if every last one of them is honest, the thief may be able to obtain information through subterfuge. He may strike up a friendship with a number of people and ask for some

Unsolicited junk mail and newspapers can be a tip-off to burglars that you're not at home. (Courtesy of John Koster.)

leads in the sales business. One thing may lead to another and he may be told, "Don't bother going over to 25 Maple . . . he's away on vacation."

Like a salesman, in fact, a burglar is always looking for leads and inside information, whether or not he actually goes out and pays for it. This applies not only to the home that the resident leaves behind but also to the hotel or motel he stays at.

At many hotels and motels, the guests are asked to leave the key to their rooms with the desk when leaving the building. This is a clear invitation to a burglar, almost too good to pass up. A clerk or anyone else working at the hotel or motel can easily sell the information about who is in (or out), provide copies of the keys, or even phone the thief at his lodgings and tell him which rooms are vacant and when the guest is expected to return.

It is inevitable that a certain amount of inside information will percolate down to the observant thief. The most important thing that a vacationer can do is to stop newspaper, mail, and milk deliveries while he is one vacation. Most newsboys and mailmen are honest, and the chance of their being dishonest is heavily outweighed by the obvious tip-off of a pile of newspapers on the front porch and a mailbox stuffed with letters. Neglecting to have mail service and newspaper delivery cancelled during a long trip amounts to putting a "Rob Me, I'm Not Home" sign on the front door.

The homeowner, however, should be very careful about whom he talks to concerning his vacation plans and, even more, where he talks about them. The fewer people you tell, the smaller the odds that a thief will find out and pay you a visit in your absence.

DEACTIVATING BURGLAR ALARMS

Most people would feel safe, even confident, if they knew they had $1,000 worth of security devices protecting their house or apartment. Electric or electronic security devices, planned by experts and installed by professional craftsmen, seem to be the ultimate barrier against unwanted visits from burglars. Unfortunately, history has shown that there is no ultimate weapon, and, like the Maginot Line, electric or electronic security devices can be bypassed by a clever and bold approach and some unorthodox thinking.

The simplest and most basic security device, of course, is the lock. Locks have existed since the ancient Egyptians built the pyramids, and thieves have been getting past them for just as long. In the days of the pharaohs, as in our own, burglary was an old and renowned profession. When Lord Carnarvon and Howard Carter discovered the tomb of King Tutankhamon in the 1920s, the excitement in the archaeological world was unparalleled, not because Tutankhamon was an important king, but because his was the first royal tomb discovered that hadn't been plundered in ancient times.

Security has improved since then, but not as much as one might think. In some cases, it has gotten worse. One pitfall of modern security is the prevalence of the slip bolt lock, which is the single most common type of lock on homes and apartments. Any thief worthy of the name can open a slip bolt lock in a few seconds with a credit card or some other strip of semirigid celluloid. The card is inserted between the door frame and the door near the lock. A strong push will force the slip bolt to open and the door follows suit.

Should the door offer stubborn resistance, or be equipped with a better-than-average lock, the thief can break in through a window, either by prying it open or simply smashing in the glass if he's sure that no one is home.

The electric devices, while they may intimidate or thwart the common amateur thief, are no real protection against the professional thief, or even against the sharper amateurs. A true story illustrates the defeat of one electric security system:

A woman in Florida spent about $500 to have a bell alarm installed on her small house. This device, when activated, would cause a loud fire-alarm-type bell to ring until either the homeowner or the police arrived at the scene. The security system installer wired up the front and back doors of the house, along with several of the most obvious windows. The bell itself was installed in a metal box fixed to the outside of the building, out of reach of anyone on the ground without the use of a ladder.

Months went by. Every few weeks, the woman would spend a few minutes testing the alarm. She wanted to make sure that the fire alarm bell was in apple-pie order.

One night, however, a burglar arrived while the woman was visiting friends and successfully plundered her home. The alarm failed to alert anyone and the thief escaped with some of her most treasured possessions and all her loose money. Disgusted at the waste of her $500 investment, she filed complaints with the installer and the manufacturer.

The thief, it turned out, had outwitted the alarm system. Before breaking into the woman's house, he had toured the grounds looking for alarm devices. When he noticed the metal box, he correctly assumed that it was only a bell alarm. Quietly, he went to her garage and removed a ladder. He set the ladder against the wall, climbed up to the bell alarm box, and methodically sprayed about three cans of shaving cream into the iron box that contained the bell. When the thief broke into the house, the alarm system had, in fact, triggered off, but the shaving cream absorbed the sound from the bell to such an extent that nobody heard it.

Had the homeowner followed up on this by removing the iron box, thus preventing the shaving cream from congealing around the bell and muffling it the next time, the thief would have simply moved one step further along and stolen the bell itself before he broke into the house. This would leave the clapper striking on empty air and producing no sound whatsoever.

Most security devices operate through the use of electricity. This is a major problem, because unless the house or apartment runs on an auxiliary generator, which turns on during a power failure, all security devices can be immobilized by cutting off the power.

Electricity can be shut off at various points. The first point in the electric power train is the switch nearest the security device. But the device itself might detect the thief before he reached it, so a more probable spot would be the fuse box in the basement. If all else fails and the thief really wants to get into the house, he may even cut a power line that feeds the entire house, which is a drastic but foolproof way to immobilize any electric-powered alarm system.

One favorite burglar alarm is a natural one—the dog. Ever since the days of the cavemen, dogs have protected their masters' homes from animal and human intruders. But thieves have ways of defeating the dog as well. Some thieves bring along two dogs with them on every job—one male and one female. When the thief encounters the homeowner's watchdog, he retreats briefly to his car and brings back his own dog, of the opposite sex. In most cases, dogs would rather be friendly with dogs of the opposite sex than attack them or interfere with human robbers, so the dogs go off to do what comes naturally while the thief does what comes naturally to *him*, and steals everything that isn't nailed down.

Other solutions to the canine problem may be less felicitous for the dog: The thief may use tranquilizers, poison, or even a bow and arrow to silence a watchdog, as happened a few years ago to a watchdog guarding an industrial site in New Jersey. Aside from discovering the failure of the dog to protect the home, the owner may experience an emotional shock at the death of his dog equal to or greater than the shock of being robbed.

USING WEATHER SIGNS

Just as darkness may favor the thief in his attempt to enter the house safely and quietly, weather conditions may help him in his quest for a dishonest dollar.

The famous quote from Herodotus that neither rain nor snow nor heat of day nor dark of night could stay the mail couriers of the Persian Empire from their appointed rounds may just as well have applied to the thieves of the Persian Empire. Certainly, there are modern thieves who don't at all object to snow and bad weather. Some of them seem to prefer it, not without reason. A true story illustrates:

A young couple who lived in an old house in Maine decided one day to brave a snowfall and visit some relatives. They took the basic precaution of leaving a light on in their house to foil burglars, and jumped into their car for a winter's jaunt. While they were out, a thief patrolled by, examined their yard, and after the usual safeguard of knocking on the door and ringing the bell, broke into the house and took what he wanted.

When the young couple returned from their jaunt to their ransacked house, they were not only shocked but confused. They couldn't understand why their house had been singled out. Unfortunately, they themselves had tipped the observant burglar off through an attempt at thrift. When leaving the house, they decided to save a little on the mounting cost of oil by turning down the heat in the house. The thief noticed this bit of frugality since the snow that piled up on the windowsills and glass hadn't melted as it would have if the heat had been turned up. Moreover, the thief—perhaps (although one hopes not) a former Boy Scout—followed the tracks that the young couple had left in the snow. There were two sets of tracks leading to the garage and none leading back—mute proof that the couple had departed and had not returned. There were also the tire tracks where the car had driven out onto the street but had not returned, and the simple fact that the car was absent furnished near-conclusive proof.

The winter wonderland that the young couple had so admired had helped lead to their undoing. Had they read *The*

Last of the Mohicans or other imaginative books about back-tracking and frontier life, they might have fooled the burglar by each leaving two tracks of footprints in the snow, walking forward and backward, and two tracks for the car by driving it in and out of the driveway and closing the garage door. Of course, this would have struck them as ridiculous at the time. But who's to say that an urban or suburban area today is any safer than the frontier was two hundred years ago? Where burglary is concerned, the suburbs may well be more danger-ous than Natty Bumpo's turf ever was.

Just as snow and ice are a congenial climate for theft, the proverbial Long Hot Summer, perhaps less surprisingly, is also conducive to crime. One thief in New Orleans liked to patrol the streets with his car windows wide open, despite the fact that his car was air-conditioned. He claimed that he could spot an empty house from blocks away, attributing this to some sixth sense. Actually, his greatest criminal asset was not a sixth sense but common sense. He cruised around looking for silent air conditioners, following up his motorized patrol-ling with some footwork. When he spotted a house which had a light on but a silent air conditioner in the window, he knew he had a probable, if not sure, target for a break-in. By leaving the air conditioner off on a hot night, the family advertised their absence just as surely as if they had turned out all the lights.

Thus the burglar would seem to have all the odds on his side: carefully acquired skills, tried and true methods, infor-mation, deliberate or inadvertent, of paid informers and in-nocent bystanders alike, and even help from the weather. At this point, the hapless homeowner or apartment dweller may be ready to throw in the sponge and yell for help. But regard-less of the odds, the burglar can be thwarted, most of the time. That's what the rest of this book is all about.

2

Buying a Home
with Security in Mind

Benjamin Franklin said in *Poor Richard's Almanac* that an ounce of prevention is worth a pound of cure. Nowhere is this more true than in the war against crime, especially for the homeowner who wants to protect himself from being burglarized. An ounce of precaution in selecting a home or apartment may be worth several thousand dollars' worth of property, if the precautions make a burglary unlikely.

When the average person considers security in buying a home, he is usually preoccupied with the safety of his person. Few people who have the money to live anywhere else buy real estate in urban slums noted for their high crime rates, any more than they buy homes next to factories or oil tank farms noted for frequent explosions. There just isn't any sense in exposing yourself unnecessarily. Unfortunately, burglary isn't restricted to slums, though it is clearly true that inner-city dwellers are the most frequent victims, as well as the most frequent perpetrators, of thefts and other crimes. Anybody can identify a slum. Identifying the calm-looking area which may be burglar-prone is a good deal more difficult. And few people bother to try. Most of them, when buying a home, are interested in the school system, the parks, the cultural life, and the convenience of shopping and perhaps mass transit. Few bother to check on the potential security problems of a town before they sign on the dotted line.

You don't have to be Sherlock Holmes or George Gallup to do some basic research on a town before you buy. A few days of work may repay you in a lifetime of burglar-free living and will be well worth the trouble. Here are some of the important facts to consider before moving in.

CRIME RATE

Every community keeps written records of the type and number of criminal violations that occur within the city limits. The record of the frequency of crime is called the *local crime rate* and is recorded in the police report. The police report, compiled daily, is released to the public annually, usually a few months after the books close at the end of the year. These police reports, sometimes called *crime rate reports*, are usually read at council meetings and given out to the press in the late winter or early spring. Copies are on file at the local clerk's office and are available for public inspection through the town clerk. Local police departments are also requested to submit copies of the police report to the Federal Bureau of Investigation. The FBI compiles these data on a nationwide basis and publishes them under the title of the *Uniform Crime Report*. This report not only supplies information on the national crime rate but breaks down the crime rate according to towns all across the nation. It is available from the U.S. Government Printing Office for about $2.85. Before the purchase of a house, the prospective homeowner should acquire either the local police report for the previous year or a copy of the *Uniform Crime Report* put out by the FBI. He can thus gain a statistically accurate picture, assuming that all crime has been reported, before he picks out a town to make a new home in.

If you obtain a copy of the *Uniform Crime Report* from the Government Prining Office, you will notice that the crime rate is given in terms of the number of crimes committed per 1,000 residents. To find the total number of given crimes committed, find out the population of the town from the municipal clerk. Divide the number of residents by 1,000, and multiply this amount by the number of crimes given in the *Uniform Crime Report*. The product will indicate the number of times last year that a given crime occurred. For example, say that according to the *Uniform Crime Report*, Johnstonville had ten burglaries per 1,000 residents. The town clerk reports that there are 50,000 residents in Johnstonville. Thus, the total number of burglaries is 500:

$$\frac{50,000 \times 10}{1,000} = 500$$

The number 500 is meaningless unless we compare the number of burglaries to that of other communities of the same size. We can also take the information contained in the *Uniform Crime Report* and determine the general chance that a resident has of being burglarized. The report stated that a burglary occurs ten times for every 1,000 residents. By dividing the number of burglaries into the number of residents, you will come out with a ratio showing the probability of being burglarized.

Thus in Johnstonville, there were ten burglaries for every 1,000 residents. You divide the number of burglaries (10) into the number of residents (1,000). This will give you one burglary per 100 residents, so that you, as a homeowner, would have one chance in 100 of being burglarized in a given town.

$$\frac{1,000}{10} = 100$$

This doesn't sound very threatening, but remember that this is the figure for a given year only. If you lived in Johnstonville for twenty-five years and the figures didn't change, your chance of being plundered would be one in four, or a 25 percent chance. If you lived there for fifty years, your chances would be 50–50. There are, however, other factors to be considered. Good security precautions can greatly reduce the odds of being plundered. Lack of security precautions can multiply the odds against the homeowner tremendously.

The most important figures in the *Uniform Crime Report*, other than the number of crimes per year, are the figures showing the percentage of increase or decrease of a given crime against the previous year's figure. Thus the same report that shows 500 burglaries in Johnstonville last year, also shows that this marks a 25 percent increase over the previous year. This is a substantial increase and may indicate a declining standard of safety in Johnstonville. A security-minded homeowner will seek a town where the crime rate has stabilized or declined rather than picking one where crime is on the increase.

The *Uniform Crime Report* uses specific law enforcement terms to categorize crime. These terms, standard ones in defining violations among law enforcement personnel, may be confusing to the layman. Here are explanations of those of interest to homeowners:

Murder and Nonnegligent Manslaughter   This crime index is defined as the willful killing of another person and is usually based solely on police investigation, as opposed to the determination of the court, medical examiner, coroner, jury, or other judicial body. Not included are deaths caused by negligence, suicide, accident, or justifiable homicide. Attempts at murder are also excluded.

Aggravated Assault   This means an actual unlawful attack by one person upon another for the purpose of inflicting bodily injury. The attack is usually accompanied by the use of a weapon or other means likely to produce death or serious injury. *Attempted aggravated assault* is usually included in this index, but *simple assault*, which may mean only a threat to commit a violent act, is not included.

Forcible Rape   This means carnal knowledge of a female through the use of force or the threat of force. Assaults in an attempt to commit forcible rape are included in this category, but *statutory rape*—intercourse with a minor when it is voluntary—is not included.

Robbery   This is a crime in which the felon obtains property in the presence of the victim by the use of force or the threat of force. *Assault to commit robbery* (mugging), *armed robbery* (a holdup with gun or knife), and attempts at all these crimes are included.

Burglary This refers to the unlawful entry into a house or other building to commit a felony or theft, even when no force is used to gain entry. In most cases, the number listed is broken down to show forcible entries, unlawful entries where no force is used, and attempted forcible entries.

Larceny–Theft This refers to the unlawful taking, or theft, of valuable articles without the use of force, violence, or fraud. This category includes such crimes as shoplifting, pocket-picking, purse-snatching, auto theft, break-ins into autos, and bicycle thefts. It does not inlcude embezzlement, con games, forgery, or worthless checks.

The definitions of the crimes listed above will enable the reader of the *Uniform Crime Report* to understand the report better. Some of the other information is also of interest. Burglary occurs about as often by day as by night, and is most frequent in the summer months of June, July, and August. The report also says that 71 percent of those arrested for burglary have been arrested previously for the same crime. For robbery, the figure is 77 percent. This high rate of recidivism, as it is called, is both an indictment of the penal system, which produces so many repeaters, and also perhaps of the legal system, since many people who have been arrested may have escaped conviction through legal chicanery. The number of experienced burglars in circulation at any one time should be a disquieting thought to any concerned homeowner.

As useful as the *Uniform Crime Report* is in determining the crime rates of various towns, there is a necessary disclaimer which must be attached to any endorsement: The *Report* is only as good as the local police work, and this varies greatly from town to town. Further, many burglaries, assaults, and other crimes go unreported. Many teenagers, and more adults than one might think, neglect to report cases of assault, especially those inspired by too much liquor. Many rapes go unreported because of embarrassment or fear on the part of the victim. And a good many burglaries are unreported, especially when no objects of great value are lost. Police officers can only make records of recorded crimes. Thus anyone reading the *Uniform Crime Report* or a local police report should assume that there may be more violations than meet the eye in any town.

POLICING THE POLICE

We learn from our earliest school days that the policeman is our friend, and in most cases he is. Thousands of people owe their lives to policemen who have rushed to their homes to administer emergency first aid to heart attack or accident victims and then sped them to the hospital in patrol cars. Police are the first line of defense against criminals and other dangers to law-abiding citizens. Their jobs, particularly in high-crime areas, are arduous, and they pay the price of their heavy responsibilities and frustrations in higher rates of suicide, divorce, heart attack, nervous breakdown, and serious digestive trouble than the population as a whole. And their pay, as a rule, is less than what people of similar ability could make elsewhere.

All this should inspire the ordinary citizen to feel respect and gratitude, but these feelings should not lead to a blind acceptance of the notion that every policeman is a good one and every police force an adequate one. Throughout American history, there have been many inept and crooked policemen and a good many police forces, past and present, rotten with corruption. This is by no means a modern phenomenon. At the turn of the century, New York Police Lieutenant Charles Becker lived high on the hog by taking rake-offs from gamblers, prostitutes, and thieves, and was ultimately executed in the electric chair at Sing Sing for ordering the murder of gambler Herman Rosenthal, who had informed against him to a crusading district attorney. In Chicago in the 1920s, bribed policemen turned their backs while gangsters shot one another down in the streets in broad daylight and beat up and threatened poll watchers on election days. One single gang reportedly paid $200,000 a year in police bribes. When Frank Loesch, a founding member of the Chicago Crime Commission, wanted to ensure an honest election in Chicago, he had to turn not to the police but to Al Capone, the head ganglord of the city, who once commented, "I own the police." As a favor to the elderly lawyer, Capone whimsically ordered an honest election, and his will was cheerfully enforced not only by his mobsters but also by the police.

These are old and extreme cases, but not totally isolated

ones. In the 1960s, local police in Mississippi were involved in the murder of civil rights workers. In South Dakota in the 1970s, Indian police were involved in election rigging, beatings, and in murders. In New York City, the famous case of Detective Frank Serpico centered on his exposure of the unbelievably widespread corruption of police; officers were involved in everything from taking bribes from gamblers and prostitutes to sleeping on the job in carefully prepared rest areas. It can be said without fear of contradiction that a blind belief in the skill and virtue of every policeman is as naïve as blind distrust of every policeman. So the cautious homeowner should make an independent evaluation of the police force guarding his prospective hometown.

The first concern is the number of police on the force. Are there enough men on the force to protect the town?

Some towns have a variety of law enforcement officers. They may be called sheriffs, constables, special police officers, police reserve, court officers, or marshals. These men are almost always part-time law enforcement personnel with a variety of limited functions such as carrying out evictions or collecting fines. Special policemen are usually men who have other full-time jobs and serve as police for short terms or in emergencies. Marshals may be detailed to directing traffic when regular police are overloaded. Many people who have these parapolice jobs are dedicated and highly qualified, while others may be totally unqualified. In the main, the interested homeowner should only consider full-time, paid policemen in his assessment of the police force.

In the *Uniform Crime Report*, the FBI suggests the proper ratio of police to residents for communities of various sizes. For a suburban community of 50,000, for instance, the FBI recommends two full-time police officers for every 1,000 residents, or a full-time force of 100. Any fewer would give the community a low-quality police service. When the police are stretched too thin, they may be unable to do their jobs properly. The police need enough people to mount motorized or foot patrols, have the desks at the police station manned, and have adequate backup personnel twenty-four hours a day.

The local police force in a well-policed town should have

standards that all members must keep. Ideally, or even minimally, all police should take formal police training at a police academy where they learn the basic skills of police work, the law, and their responsibilities, and where people who are clearly unfit for police work can be weeded out. In the past, and even at present, too many ordinary people become policemen merely by pinning on a badge and strapping on a gun. All too often, these untrained men lack the skills or the "psychology" to be good policemen. In recent years, many forces have begun to grant scholarships and pay incentives to officers to take college courses in police-related skills. These may include not only relevant basics such as the law, narcotics abuse, and police science, but courses in related fields such as psychology and sociology. The homeowner should inquire about such courses and find out what sort of program exists in his prospective town.

Police officers should be in relatively good shape physically and neat and professional in appearance and attitude. A visit to the police station can be used to check on these matters, which may be more important than they seem. A police force in which everybody is overage and overweight probably won't do much legwork or patrolling, and a sloppy attire may mean low morale or lackadaisical professional standards.

Last, but not least, police should be reasonably well paid. Poorly paid policemen may have to moonlight to make ends meet at home, and a policeman who spends all day painting somebody else's living room, hanging wallpaper, or mowing lawns may be inclined to drive the patrol car into some shady nook and take a nap instead of patrolling on his night shift. Moreover, good pay tends to attract people of high abilities, and poor pay does just the reverse. Of course, it is possible to find skilled and dedicated policemen on forces that pay badly, but the odds are all against it.

Once having checked out the town in the *Uniform Crime Report* or in the local police report, the homeowner should visit the police station to inspect the force and also ask to see a roster of the patrolmen. Most small towns have a roster readily available. There are two factors to look at here. The first is to try to ascertain if all the town's various ethnic groups are represented on the roster. A town with an uneven balance of any one group on the force may be a trouble spot because of tensions inherent in letting one group do all the policing. The kind of tension that can build up when, for instance, a town with a substantial black or Hispanic or Indian population has an all-white police force is easily understood. The groups not represented may tend to regard the all-white police force almost as an occupation army, and may not cooperate with the police. This sort of resentment can build revolt, especially among youngsters, who may turn to vandalism or petty burglary in an outburst of protest.

The second important factor is nepotism, which has been the ruin of a good many police forces. There are towns, especially in rural areas, where the police roster will look like the mayor's or police chief's family tree. This may mean that a great many uninterested and unqualified men are entering the force because it's an easy living, and can lead to great resentment by nonrelatives who are passed over for promotion.

A story from a town in New Jersey illustrates how nepotism and inattention to duty virtually crippled a police force. The chief detective in a New Jersey town worked the night shift—in theory, at least—because this was when most crime was expected to take place. By day, the detective was a partner in a stock brokerage investigative firm. He was supposed to determine the value of old stocks and bonds and report back to clients in writing. Since he was the police chief's brother-in-law, nobody ever called him on the carpet, even when it was common knowledge that he wrote up the stock brokerage reports from his daytime job while he was on duty at night. In fact, the detective was so busy working at his spare job that he never had time to be a sleuth, and the town was left without a functioning chief detective day and night.

This led to low morale all through the department. The men felt it was useless to work hard since only family members got ahead anyway. The whole force went slack and did as little as humanly possible. Bad morale ultimately came to mean bad police work, and thus bad protection for the homeowner. Nepotism, in this case, was at the root of the problem. There have, of course, been many cases in which a father and several of his sons have been policemen and have done excellent jobs, but evidence of nepotism should at least cause the homeowner to investigate further to see if the morale or efficiency of the force has been impaired.

Police morale is obviously important, and there are considerations other than nepotism to think about. There is a general pattern in the career of a police officer which parallels most other jobs. When a young officer joins the force, he may go through a shakedown period in which he is ill at ease and has a lot to learn. After this period of about a year, he usually goes through a period of five years or so at peak efficiency, in which his energy and performance are high. After this, especially in a small suburban department, the policeman's performance and morale will often decrease because of lack of job opportunity and advancement. The small police force only has jobs for so many sergeants and detectives, and since the turnover is small, some patrolmen may wait as long as twelve years for their first promotion. Their interest in their work may decline in these interim years.

The prospective homeowner should try to meet several policemen on a personal basis to try to assess for himself the morale of the force. Though direct questioning may not be a good idea, and may prove unproductive, an astute listener can usually pick up the basic morale pattern of the force by some casual talks with the patrolmen. Conversations with local merchants and ordinary citizens can also sometimes provide a balanced picture of police efficiency and morale, provided that the merchants and citizens aren't strongly biased for or against police in general.

The final checkup on police efficiency should come through direct observation.

The most important function of the police, at least from the homeowner's point of view, is patrolling. The police patrol is the strongest defense that individual departments have against burglars and other felons. The very word "cop," in fact, is supposed to stem from "Constable on Patrol." Police are usually assigned to patrol the town in sections, with each man and car assigned to a specific beat. The cars are supposed to drive through each street at least twice per shift, not usually at a scheduled time, but at irregular intervals, so that a thief cannot wait until the patrol passes and then assume he has two hours of safety to work on the outside of a house.

A prospective homeowner can check the patrols by remaining near the site of his intended house and observing whether or not the police patrols pass by. Needless to say, you had better take a good book because this is time-consuming. You will have to stay at least three successive nights to gain any fair idea of patrol tactics, since the police are subject to emergency calls and might justifiably miss a sweep once in a while because of more important business elsewhere.

Ideally, the patrol car should pass each location in town often enough to observe any unusual conditions on the block. The patrol officer should question persons who don't seem to have business in that part of the community, including those sitting in parked cars or loitering on street corners.

If the homeowner doesn't see a police patrol at all for a few nights, he should ask about this at the police station. Some towns patrol at night by simply parking the cars in strategic locations and watching traffic while waiting for emergency calls on the radio. Unfortunately, this has the effect of not doing much to discourage burglars and other felons or loiterers. At night, the policeman may even go to sleep at the wheel of the car. Needless to say, this isn't the protection you're paying for. A wide-awake police force is a strong line of defense against burglary. A police force asleep on the job is a bad bargain at any price.

OTHER INFORMATION

A broad range of information is the key to selecting a good hometown. One of the best sources of information is apt to be the local newspaper. A prospective resident should regularly read the local paper for the town he is considering. The paper will furnish news about crimes, which can be incorporated with the *Uniform Crime Report* and police information to give a current picture of the community's crime rate. Moreover, the newspaper will describe social and political events of the town and give a balanced picture of what it is like to live there.

Many papers, however, neglect to print news of minor crimes. A good source of additional information is municipal court. Municipal courts usually convene twice a month, and all criminal cases which occur are heard there, with the more serious cases referred to grand juries at the county seat or elsewhere. You can find out when municipal court sessions are scheduled from the local police and attend a few sessions. Most of the cases that appear will probably be motor vehicle violations, but if a significant proportion of burglaries or other felonies are tried, this may be an indication of a heavy concentration of crime. Of course, it may also mean that the police force is on their toes, and is catching the perpetrators instead of letting them slip through their fingers. Nevertheless, municipal court is a good place to assess the sort of "local color" that doesn't turn up at garden parties or town council meetings.

Your future neighbors may turn out to be your best source of information about the town you are interested in. Talking to local merchants, the chamber of commerce, local politicians, and the municipal clerk may help give you a more balanced picture of your prospective home than the one you got from the real estate man. Discernment should be exercised. Old people will often say that things aren't the way they used to be, just as young people almost always think the town they live in is dull. But casual conversations may turn up some good information.

One of the best but most frequently overlooked sources of information about a town is the local reporter who covers the town for his newspaper. The homeowner can usually find one or more reporters at a town council meeting or municipal court. Failing this, he can call the newspaper and ask which reporter covers the town in question. Most reporters are naturally garrulous and will generally give a picture of a given town unclouded by local pride or defensiveness. Since they often cover more than one town, they can offer a good com-

Because thieves sometimes pose as salesmen, many towns require door-to-door salesmen to register with police and carry identification cards. This gentleman wears one on his lapel. (Courtesy of John Koster.)

parative picture of which towns in the region are good security risks—off the record, of course.

LOCAL AND STATE LAWS

State laws and municipal ordinances differ from one town to another, and there are no nationwide codes governing certain aspects of commerce. In some cases, laws or the lack of laws concerning door-to-door peddlers may play into the hands of burglars, who, as we have seen, often go around knocking on doors to find out if anyone is home and pose as door-to-door salesmen if a resident answers the door. Some burglars even come equipped with business cards, order blanks, and samples, in case they misjudge a target and find a resident at home.

To put a damper on this kind of foil, many towns have adopted laws requiring all door-to-door canvassers to register with the police. Under this law, anyone who intends to canvass a town, whether for charity or for sales purposes, has to report to the police station. Here his fingerprints will be checked and police will send the prints to the state police or FBI to find out if he has a criminal record. They will also check up to find out if the company he claims to represent actually exists, or if the charity he claims to represent is a bona fide nonprofit organization. Sometimes the solicitor is also asked to post a cash bond which will be returned when he leaves town. Under most circumstances, the investigation takes about a week, and if the salesman passes muster, he will be issued an identification card, often displaying his photograph and the signature of the police chief. This card should be presented to every homeowner spontaneously or on demand.

The prospective homeowner should find out if this law is in effect in the community he hopes to live in. Many communities have such laws. A few ban soliciting entirely. Either law will cut down on burglaries because the would-be burglar will be unable to pose as a door-to-door salesman or fund solicitor. The existence of this ordinance or law is a good argument in favor of moving to a town. The lack of it is a good argument for thinking twice before you move there. Honest salesmen and sincere do-gooders won't object to having their snapshots taken, or even to being fingerprinted, a process that is absolutely painless, if somewhat smudgy. Every man who joins the armed forces and every legal immigrant is fingerprinted, and many companies also insist on taking fingerprints of their employees. The process can hardly be said to impose an undue hardship on anyone but a burglar.

Another law that helps thwart burglary is a ban on on-street parking during the late night and early morning hours. A burglar who is working a neighborhood generally keeps his car nearby for a fast getaway. If he makes his car conspicuous by parking it on the street during a parking ban, the police on patrol can readily spot the car and find out who's driving it. Experienced criminals know this and avoid towns with on-street parking bans. Of course, this may cause some slight inconvenience if you're having a party and can't find room for all your friends in the driveway, but a call to the police station will generally result in permission for a one-night relaxation on enforcement. In general, the ban on late night parking is well worth any inconvenience it may cause. The prospective homeowner should find out not only whether such laws are on the books but whether they are routinely enforced. If the laws are down on paper but not enforced, they won't deter the burglar one iota.

SECURITY OF THE HOUSE

Once you've determined whether the community you're considering is a good security risk, you should give your new prospective house some individual attention. A good sound house is an essential of security, even in the safest of towns with the best of police forces.

Your first inspection of the house should begin in daylight hours. Take a tour of the grounds and check whether you can see both the front and the sides of the house from the street— the place from which police routinely make their surveillance. There should be no shrubbery, hedges, trees, statuary, or other obstructions blocking a full view of the doors and windows from the street or sidewalk. If you're buying the house in the winter or early spring, you should consider the possible effect that full leaf and bloom will have on the shrubbery and trees. Obviously, you may be able in January to peer through the thin whiplike branches of some trees and shrubs and get a clear view of the doors and windows, while the fully leaved branches will form an impenetrable curtain in July or August—the months when burglary is most frequent. Don't let a love of nature or a concern with shade make you a sitting duck for a burglar.

After the day inspection, make a similar inspection at night. Lack of adequate street or house lighting may turn what looks like a clearly visible front door by daylight into a mysterious portal at the end of a gloomy tunnel. Your prospective house and the houses around it should be clearly illuminated at all times, especially near the doors and lower windows.

After an on-site inspection, talk to the local police about a house before buying. Police know that some houses are burglarprone, and the former owner may even be moving because the house has been hit too many times. The real estate sales people may not volunteer such information, so check with police, and, if possible, with neighbors as well as with the former residents and salespeople. Buying a house that is prone to burglary and that neighborhood thieves know as a local landmark can be as foolish as buying a house with a leaky roof or termites.

The next step calls for a little bit of playing Sherlock Holmes. Insist on a slow tour of the premises with the real estate agent or owner and take a look around for signs of burglar activity. Check all exterior doors and windows for marks of forcible entry. To do this, look for areas where the doors or windows are locked or latched, and see if there are any chipped pieces of wood on the frame or dents as if made with a flat knife blade or chisel. Broken panes of glass, or new panes set among old ones, are also possible signs of forcible entry or vandalism. You should check every door and pane of window glass before completing your tour.

Take note of the security system which the present or former owner has installed in the house. A special lock on first-floor windows, special locks or chains on the door, and any other evidence of extra security precautions may indicate a previous burglar or attempted entry, and you should ask some probing questions if you find any of these devices on your prospective home. The seller must have had a reason to install such added precautions.

New doors or new windows may also be a symptom of a burglar-prone house. Wear and tear may account for new doors and windows, but burglary shouldn't be ruled out either.

Check with a local insurance agent to determine the annual premium for home insurance on a house like the one in question and especially for burglar and vandal insurance. Find out what the average premium is, and then find out what the premium would be if the owner of the home had filed several theft claims. When you have this information, ask the owner of the house what he is paying as his annual insurance premium. Based on the information you have from the insurance agent, you'll be able to make a pretty educated guess as to whether the house has been burglarized.

There's an old saying about lightning not striking twice, but it doesn't hold true for houses plagued by burglars or vandals. Vandals sometimes select a homeowner for continual harassment, often for the most capricious reasons: he may be of a different race or religion, he may be known for his bad disposition, or his house may merely be situated along a route that children use for shortcuts to and from school or the playground. Some people have had glass lanterns or signs broken so many times, flowerpots smashed so often, or graffiti painted on their walls and sidewalls so frequently that they don't even bother to repair the damage—except when trying to sell the house. When they do sell the house, it may not make any difference to the vandals whether they have moved or not. The house may still be a target.

LIGHTING

The house you purchase should be properly lit to repel burglars. This is especially true of the house located in the middle of the block, away from street corners, the favored target of the night burglar.

Tour the vicinity of the house after dark—after letting the owner know that you're coming, unless you yourself want to be picked up as a burglar. If there's enough light to illuminate all doors and ground-floor windows, you're all right. Spotlights aren't necessary for adequate security. Even a 30-watt standard light bulb is all right if it lights the side of the house well enough to let anyone on the street detect a prowler. There should also be enough light to let a next-door neighbor see if the strange noise he or she heard in the backyard was made by a cat or a burglar. If the present lights on the house are inadequate, you will have to bear the cost of adding more lights when you move in. On the other hand, if the house is spotlighted like a Hollywood sound stage, it may have been burglarized in the past, and lights may represent an attempt to ward off future burglars.

Because of the high cost of electricity and the energy crisis in general, excessive lighting is probably as undesirable as inadequate lighting. For the average house, only four outdoor fixtures are necessary—one on each side, with a 30- or 50-watt bulb. This may not be enough light to read the fine print in the mortgage by, but it will make any thief feel uncomfortable about spending much time huddled next to your house. Needless to say, all the lighting in the world won't help if tall shrubbery or other obstructions give the thief something to hide behind. The exterior lighting system of the house should also contain an automatic light switch, not a manual switch. The switch should operate according to the amount of illumination in the area, so that if the homeowner should leave home and be late in returning, he won't tip off a burglar as to his absence by leaving the outside lights off.

SUMMARY

To simplify the somewhat involved process of making a security check when a new home is being chosen, here is a checklist of the points to consider in selecting a new home. The new homeowner shouldn't hesitate to assert himself and ask questions before buying a house. A house is the major investment most people will make in a lifetime, and choosing one that is a security asset, rather than a risk, may result in a great saving of money and aggravation.

Here are the points to check:

1. Local crime rate according to the *Uniform Crime Report.*
2. Number of burglaries last year.
3. Number of aggravated assaults.
4. Number of forcible rapes.
5. Number of robberies.
6. Number of larceny–thefts.
7. Number of auto thefts.
8. What are your chances of becoming a victim of these crimes?
9. How many full-time police officers should the town have, according to FBI standards?
10. How many does the town in fact have now?
11. What are the local police department's training standards?
12. Is there a nepotism problem in the department?
13. Was the police chief questioned about the town and were his answers good?

14. What does the morale in the department seem to be?

15. Were police officers questioned? Were they alert, polite, and intelligent?

16. Were police patrols checked three times a day? By day? At night?

17. What are the local newspapers like?

18. Did you purchase these papers on a regular basis?

19. Did you attend municipal court and check on the type of crimes?

20. Did you talk to merchants, neighbors, the chamber of commerce, local politicians, and the municipal clerk?

21. Did you talk to local reporters?

22. Does the community permit on-street overnight parking?

23. Does the community require a permit to solicit door-to-door?

24. Can you see the front and sides of the house from the opposite sides of the street?

25. Is the foliage in full bloom?

26. Can you see the front door and first-floor windows from the street?

27. Does the house look vacant?

28. Were the police asked about previous crime problems in the house and neighborhood?

29. Did you take a slow tour of the outside and inside of the house?

30. Were there any signs of forced entry around the windows and doors?

31. Were there any special locks around the doors and windows?

32. Are there any new windows and doors?

33. What is the average insurance premium for burglary and vandal insurance in the area?

34. What would the premium be if several claims had been made?

35. What is the present owner of the house paying?

36. Are there lights around the house exterior?

37. What is the wattage of the bulbs?

38. Does the light switch activate by illumination?

3

Is Your House Inviting a Burglar?

Life being what it is, not everybody can afford to go shopping for a new house just because the old homestead may not be exactly burglarproof. Most people, in fact, will have to make do with the house they already have, and the same precautions that one should take when buying a new house apply when one is burglarproofing an existing house.

First and perhaps foremost, of course, is the issue of total visibility of the front and sides of the house from the street. This is essential to discourage burglars from trying to hide near the house and break in. The homeowner should assure himself of a clear line of sight from the street to the house.

The most frequent obstructions to a clear view are trees and shrubbery. For instance, a 6- or 7-foot hedge may make the front of your house totally invisible from the street. If this is the case, you should trim the hedge down to 3 feet, which will probably give anyone on the street a clear view. Low-hanging limbs of trees should be trimmed, preferably by a tree surgeon who knows how to lop off limbs without harming the tree.

Good landscaping is important for another reason. If the lawn is neatly trimmed, the hedge cropped, and things around the yard generally shipshape and Bristol fashion, it will give the house a neat, lived-in appearance. A lawn that hasn't been mowed in weeks is almost as good as a tip-off that nobody's home as a stack of letters jammed in the mailbox or a heap of newspapers on the doorstep.

An additional reason for keeping your house visible has nothing to do with burglary but everything to do with safety. There may be a time when a police car or an ambulance has to answer an emergency call at your house—a heart attack, a serious accident, a prowler, or some other major problem— and maybe a precious life—your life, or that of a loved one— may be lost. Less crucial than this, but perhaps more commonplace, is the aggravation that friends may endure when trying to find your house at night if they aren't familiar with the neighborhood. So keeping your front yard neat and your house front visible and well lighted can have added benefits.

You may even want to go across the street and take a picture

Front yard foliage partly obscures the front of this house, making a thief's job easier. (Courtesy of Mike SanGiovanni.)

of your house front to study at your leisure. In this way you can plan a landscaping job that will give your house an attractive appearance while leaving the front visible at all times.

EXTERIOR LIGHTING

As has been said, exterior lighting of the house is an extremely important deterent to burglars. A dark exterior is an invitation to an unexpected visit, but by casting a little light on the subject, the homeowner may save himself a lot of loss and aggravation.

If you're at all handy with tools and know a little bit about electricity you can do it yourself. You don't have to hire an electrician to come out and set up floodlights around your house so that it looks like Graumann's Chinese Theater on the night of the big premiere. This kind of lighting can have its bad points. For one thing, the electric bills are apt to be astronomical. For another, too many lights may annoy your neighbors or even you. One man in New Jersey who paid for all sorts of lighting around his impressive colonial-style house quickly regretted his decision when people he had never seen before began to drive into his driveway and right up to the door and expect to be seated in the dining room. His house was so conspicuous that they had assumed it was a restaurant.

Unless you want to make some money yourself serving the specialty of the house, this kind of lighting is superfluous. You can get equal protection, and less annoyance and expense, from a half-dozen 30-watt outdoor light bulbs installed in simple outdoor light sockets. You should have one bulb set to illuminate the front door and another one over the ground-floor windows, half shaded so as not to disturb your neighbors or people on the upstairs floor of the house. The light should not be placed directly over the window, however, and it should not be within easy reach of the ground. If it is, the thief may just reach up, unscrew it, and continue his burglary in total darkness.

The 30-watt light bulbs may not seem impressive, but you don't have to have enough light to read fine print by to dissuade burglars. Look at it this way: If the wall of your house were the backstop of a carnival shooting gallery, would there

The front of the house is reasonably clean-cut and offers good visibility of the door from the street. (Courtesy of Mike SanGiovanni.)

In contrast to this house's clean-cut front (above), the side is cluttered and obscure, making it easy for a thief to hide in the bushes if police approach. (Courtesy of Mike SanGiovanni.)

be enough light to make the burglar an easy target? If there would be, the burglar may see it that way, too.

The back door, any side doors, and the door of the attached garage, if there is one, should be illuminated along the same lines as the front of the house. Again, make sure that the light bulbs can't be reached and unscrewed from ground level or by climbing a tree. Most burglars don't walk around with ladders, so if you yourself need a ladder to change light bulbs, they are probably safe from burglars.

INTERIOR LIGHTING

The subject of interior lighting, that is, the normal house lights, is one for which there is no exact rule. The most salient fact, of course, is that if a burglar suspects that you're at home he won't try to break in. One of the best ways to convince him that you're home is to leave lights on.

The question is, how many lights?

A completely dark house during normal home-life hours, that is, from dusk to 11 or 11:30 P.M., is a simple invitation to burglary. You might as well put a "Rob Me, I'm Not Home" sign on your front door as leave your house completely blacked out before bedtime. Leaving the house completely dark is asking for trouble.

If you leave a single light on, preferably in the living room or other ground-floor room close to the front door, where it's readily visible from the street, the chances are fair that a burglar won't bother to investigate further. Peering through somebody's window after dark, in times like these, is a good way to get your face shot off, or at least to prompt hysterical screams for help and calls to the police. Nevertheless, more and more people are learning the elementary trick of leaving a single light on, so burglars are becoming more discriminating. Some of them, if they have any other reason to suspect that no one is home, will keep an eye on a house where only a single light is burning, and, if they don't see any lights go on or off for some time, they may risk ringing the doorbell with a phony salesman pitch, or at least make a phone call. The trick is so well known that some burglars leave their lights burning to ward off other burglars.

One alternative to this ploy is to leave a light burning in every room of the house. Unfortunately, this will run up an unbearable electric bill, and may even prompt the burglar to investigate further since a house that is lit up like a carnival but doesn't show any overt signs of life may be a curiosity. So turning on every light in the house, besides being expensive, is apt to be self-defeating.

One good light to leave on, besides the one in the living room, is the bathroom light, if it shows on the street. The sight of this light will usually convince the burglar that somebody is up with indigestion, a hangover, cramps, or some other midnight misery, and this will probably dissuade him from investigation.

To augment the lights, a good trick if you only step out briefly, is to leave on the TV or, better yet, the radio, turned up loud enough to be audible outside your home, yet not loud enough to disturb neighbors or make an unseemly racket. If the burglar should investigate and hear the noises the radio or TV is making, he may think that what he hears is you and your family talking. At worst, he will assume that somebody is home listening to the music, and this will dissuade him from entering.

Perhaps the most foolproof trick of all, other than hiring a crew of actors to impersonate you and your family, is to purchase one or more light timers and set them up to simulate the activities of people at home. Light timers usually cost about $5.00 at the hardware store, and screw into the light sockets between the lamp and the bulb. They can be set to turn your lights on and off at preset times. With a little of that old James Bond ingenuity, you can get one or two timers to duplicate your movements around the house. For instance, if you usually go to the kitchen for a snack before bedtime, you might set the living room timer to snap off at 11:00 P.M. and the kitchen timer to turn the light on at 10:30. This will ensure that nothing looks fishy, even if the synchronization of the two timers isn't exact. Work out your own schedule based on the way you live: you may want to leave the bathroom light on all night, and set the living room timer to snap on at 6:30 and off at 11:30 or midnight.

One thing is almost certain: If the burglar sees one light on, other lights blinking on and off, and can hear noises or music coming from your house—and, of course, if you don't have a huge stack of letters, bills, and newspapers jammed in your mailbox or an empty garage staring out at the street—he'll probably decide that your place isn't worth any more investigation.

GARAGE ENTRANCE

Your garage may be many things: a shelter for your family car, a storage depot for paint, rags, and garden tools, a breeding ground for stray cats, a roost for bats, or a sacrosanct repository for your 45-year-old collection of *Liberty* and *Saturday Evening Post* magazines. It may also be the easiest way into your house for an enterprising burglar.

Some time ago, a couple with two children decided to go on a vacation trip. Before they left, they made a security check on the home. The newspaper and milk delivery were stopped, and so was the mail service. The couple set timers on several lamps to simulate their presence. The timers were arranged in sequence to make it look as if the family were walking around switching lights on and off. Before they left, the husband checked all the doors and windows and thought he had left nothing to chance. They left for their trip with high hearts and no worries.

Unfortunately, when the family got back they found their house a shambles and some of their valuables gone. A thief had paid them an unwanted visit despite their precautions.

Subsequent investigation showed that the thief had taken a big chance and practiced his door-to-door selling ploy. When no one answered after he knocked and rang, he was sure that there was no one home and that he could break in. Note here that, if the radio had been left turned up fairly loud, he might have thought that his ringing and knocking hadn't been heard, and thought twice about proceeding. The dead silence tipped him off.

It was the method that the burglar used to gain entry that came as something of a surprise. The burglar simply went to the door of the attached garage, opened it—the owner hadn't locked it—and walked right into the house. Dead bolt locks on the main doors might have saved the house from forcible entry except for the unlocked garage door.

An attached garage is a convenience in rainy weather or darkness. It fosters the illusion many people seem to have that their car is really an extension of their house, and that they can climb right into the auto and still be "at home." Unfortunately, an attached garage is a frequent avenue of forcible entry. In the true story above, the thief found the garage open, which made it especially easy for him to loot the house, even though a locked garage presents no real obstacle. Had the garage door been locked, he could have plastered the window with a few strips of masking tape and then broken the glass with a good firm blow. This masking tape technique enables the burglar to shatter the window with a minimum of noise and without scattered shards of glass. The glass breaks not with a loud shattering sound but with a sort of dull crunch.

Locking the wheels, even if the bike is stored in a garage, may be a good idea. (Courtesy of Master Lock Co.)

Thieves don't often use the trick to break into a house that may have people inside, since it may cause them to walk in on somebody who just happens to be cleaning a gun, stirring his fireplace with a hot poker, or playing cards with three football teammates, all of which could prove embarrassing. The trick works just fine on structures that aren't likely to be occupied, such as storefronts or garages.

Once he's inside the garage, the thief can take his own sweet time about breaking into the main house. The garage provides him with a made-to-order hiding place, and most people don't lock the doors between the house and the garage, any more than they lock the door between the kitchen and the living room.

If the door should be locked, the thief has less of a problem than he would elsewhere. He may even have a splendid array of tools to choose from to complete the break-in. Since most

This covered porch offers good shelter to a burglar intent on picking the main door lock, which is on the door inside the porch, unseen here—and from the street. (Courtesy of Mike SanGiovanni.)

A house with clear sides makes a thief's job more difficult. Shrubs near the door could stand a trimming. (Courtesy of Mike SanGiovanni.)

families keep their tool chest in the garage—displayed neatly, perhaps, on a perforated beaverboard on the wall, like dinosaur eggs at the Museum of Natural History—the burglar can pick and choose just what he wants to get through the door. If you have power tools in the garage, he can probably cut a new door through the wall for you, given time and incentive. For good measure, of course, he may even steal the tools.

Thus an adjacent garage can be a real Achilles' heel to your home security program. If you have one, you should take the same or greater precautions with the attached garage that you take with the rest of the house. You should have dead bolt locks on both doors—the one leading into the garage from outside and the one from the garage to the house. It's better not to have any windows on the garage door or the garage itself, since these are a prime source of illegal entry. If the windows are desired, or if they're already there and can't be helped, keep them well illuminated. By all means, make sure that the burglar can't just break a window in the door and then reach in and open the latch. And never, ever leave a garage door open when you go out shopping.

The same, of course, holds true for any attached patios or enclosed porches, which shelter a burglar while he breaks into the main door. If you have an enclosed porch, make sure that the outer door is just as strong and the lock just as good as the one that separates the porch from the house.

BACK DOORS

The back door poses some special problems. For openers, it can't be seen from the street, so the thief usually has a little more leisure time to fool around with the locks than he would if trying to pry open a well-lit front door.

The back door, too, is quite often sheltered by a small awning or roof. This is nice and convenient when bringing home the groceries in a rainstorm. It's also nice and convenient for the burglar who can log some real time picking the back door while the awning shelters him from view from adjacent houses.

Lastly, there is another foible of homeowners that plays right into the thief's hands. Most people wouldn't think of leaving the key to the front door atop the doorjamb or under the milkbox, but the back door seems so much more . . . personal . . . so homey . . . so they leave the key in some obvious place, the thief finds it in thirty seconds of determined searching, and he gets in and plunders the house.

So you have several things to be done if you want to have a secure house. The first, which may seem somewhat drastic, is to remove any awning or roof that obscures the back door from the view of the neighbors and to make sure that it is properly lit. If you need a rain screen, you can use clear plastic that will stop the rain but not the surveillance of the police or neighbors.

Second, you can remove the key from its obvious hiding place and make sure that the thief can't get at it. Put it on your keyring. Tape it inside your wallet or purse where you can reach it if you have to. Put a spare in your car's glove compartment—and change it immediately if someone steals your car. But *don't* leave the key lying around where any burglar or juvenile or foraging raccoon may expose it to view with a random step—and, in the case of the thief, use it to get inside your house and plunder it.

Since the back door is in the weakest position as far as street surveillance goes, you may want to install some extra warning devices. This doesn't mean splurging on the latest James Bond gadgetry or trying to set up an electronic system designed to cope with Hunt and Liddy. One device that will shake up the ordinary burglar is quite simple and extremely cheap. Save up a dozen or so tin cans and find or purchase a thin slab of wood, say, maybe a piece of plywood 1 foot broad and 2 feet long. When you're going to leave for an absence of any duration and don't intend to use the back door to get back in, lock the door. Then stick the piece of plywood between the door and the overhead doorframe like a shelf, and pile up the tin cans in a stack on the plywood plank. If anyone jimmies your door open or even shakes it, the cans will come falling down like an armored knight falling off his charger, and the burglar probably won't stop running until he's in the next county. Even if he isn't frightened off, he should be, because the clangor will probably wake up one or more of your neighbors.

A variation of the same trick is to string out a half dozen tin cans on a wire and drape them across the back door on the inside out of sight. Put a few pebbles or dry beans in each can. This simple detection system was used in World War I, when the soldiers used it to make sure that nobody crawled through the barbed wire entanglements in front of their trenches to surprise them. The grenade traps used in the same era are interesting, too, but not suitable to home security unless you happen to live in a pillbox.

Another pitfall to some older homes is a crawl space with a window that opens onto a window on the outside of the house. The inside entry to this crawl space may lead to a staircase or someplace in the cellar. These crawl spaces have their uses—many were built as coalbins—but they are a security hazard and nuisance of prime magnitude. An enterprising burglar can break or jimmy the window, crawl through the crawl space, come out in the basement, and then simply walk up the staircase, enter the house, and do what comes naturally. If your house is plagued with such a nuisance, brick it up immediately. If you can't do that, keep the window locked, lock the door to your cellar from the upstairs side with a dead bolt and/or a chain, and hope for the best. One trick, if you don't plan on moving, is to fill the crawl space with broken glass, which will deter any burglar who isn't a masochist. When you break a glass in the kitchen, don't throw it in the garbage can—throw it into the crawl space. Burglars aren't delirious about crawl spaces because they don't like spiders more than the average person does. If you sour the pot with the additional danger of being cut up by broken glass, most of them won't try to make a subterranean attack.

INFORMING THE NEIGHBORS

The average thief is an opportunist of the first water. Few people feel a vocational calling to crime the way some people want to write or paint or do social work. Thus the thief, like all too many other people, will always take the line of least resistance. He'll try to break into almost any house, no matter how meager the pickings may be, provided that he's reasonably sure he can do so without getting caught.

Padlocks may be useful in securing movable property or in emergency situations when regular locks are broken. This one stopped a bullet from a .44 magnum. (Courtesy of Master Lock Co.)

The only way a thief can be caught—unless you come home and find him at work, which can be dangerous—is if he is spotted by police or by a neighbor who calls the police. Even the best police force can't be everywhere at once, so your neighbors may well be the main distant early warning line against burglars.

In many neighborhoods, the people next door hear music from your house quite often—perhaps more often than you realize. If you like the Grateful Dead or Moby Grape and they dig Beethoven and Bach, this can be mutually unpleasant. More often than most of us realize, the neighbors may also hear arguments between the adjacent husband and wife, or the disciplining of the little angels, both of which can prove embarrassing. Most people are decent enough not to let on how much they actually know about what goes on next door, which is probably a good thing for all concerned.

There is one advantage to this proximity. If the guy next door can hear you and the little woman going at it, or the Rolling Stones blasting away on your radio, he can also make out the sound of a burglar kicking in your front door or lofting a brick through your window. The problem is, will your neighbor report this to the police?

In recent years, psychologists and others have become more and more concerned with the problem of alienation. It seems that in many neighborhoods, people just don't relate to one another and prefer to remain totally aloof and isolated. In New York and in other big cities, people can be seen stepping nonchalantly over bodies on the sidewalk as if they were logs or bags of garbage, ignoring the recumbent figures. These prostrate figures may be drunks or drug users, or they may just as easily be normal, respectable people who have fainted because of heart attack or been felled by muggers. Nobody wants to get involved. People who come from small towns and see this may react like recruits facing their first battle. The classic story of New York apathy was that of Kitty Genovese, a waitress who was stabbed to death while screaming for help in full earshot of dozens of her neighbors, who listened without trying to help, without calling the police.

This kind of alienation is a marked contrast to the strong feelings of some people who live in small towns and to the residents of some of the older ethnic neighborhoods. People who have lived in the same neighborhood for two or three generations or those with roots in the Old World often have a strong feeling of kinship. When a baby is born, when someone dies, or when a major event takes place, everybody on the block knows about it. This kind of society, of course, has its faults—provincial outlooks, limited horizons and ambitions, and sometimes strong prejudice against other ethnic groups. But from the security standpoint, people in the close-knit neighborhood are better off.

In the alienated neighborhood, it is not unknown for a neighbor to come forward during the investigation and admit that he or she heard strange noises while the burglary was in progress, but didn't think anything of it—or do anything about it. Needless to say, this admission didn't do the homeowner who was plundered any good.

How much better would it be, even if the neighbors know one another only casually, to work out a verbal agreement to call the police if they hear or see anything definitely suspicious? This doesn't involve any risk-taking. In most cases, all the neighbor has to do is call police headquarters and say, "There's something suspicious going on at 32 Oak Street." Police probably won't even ask his name or address if he sounds like a responsible adult. If they are alert, however, they will send one or more patrol cars to the scene in time to frighten the burglar away or even to capture him. Thus the neighbor helps protect the neighborhood at no risk to himself and with very little effort.

Community spirit not only will help deter burglary but will make life more rewarding in general. Nobody is suggesting a return to vigilantism or urging people to form a posse and ride out in search of evildoers to lynch. But by serving as eyes and ears for the police in protection of their own and their neighbor's property, conscientious homeowners can cut down the astronomical costs of crime with no risk to themselves.

SIMILAR LAYOUTS

Suppose, after all your precautions, that a burglar should break into your house. He will find a strange environment, one which he hasn't seen before. His major concern, once inside, is to find your valuables, gather them up, and flee before being detected. Experience will have taught him the usual places that people keep their most treasured possessions: drawers in the bedroom are the favored places, along with bedroom closets. The only problem the burglar has is locating the bedroom and guessing which closets to look into.

His problem may be eliminated if you live a housing development where all the houses are basically laid out on the same plan: living room behind the front door, master bedroom off to one side, etc. If the thief has broken into one house in the development, he knows the floor plan and can follow through. The same is true if he breaks into an apartment building in which all the apartment units are arranged in the same way.

Designers of developments realize this, and in recent years they have begun to vary the construction of houses in their developments, so that each house is laid out a bit differently from its neighbor. Of course, they tend to repeat patterns on a grander scale so that each block of a dozen houses may be symmetrical. But varying the layout from house to house may confuse the burglar. By living in such a development, instead of one in which every house is laid out in exactly the same fashion, the homeowner can cut the odds against a successful burglary by a small degree.

The homeowner can also make the burglar's life a little more difficult by adapting his living habits to a layout different than the one the designer may have intended. Of course it's impractical to move your master bedroom furniture into the bathroom or set up your kitchen in the basement. But storing your possessions in unorthodox places may help save them if a burglar should break in. One trick is to get a mason jar, paint the inside with white paint, and use it to store household money in the refrigerator—"cold cash," as one homeowner calls it. With a change in paint color, you can use a mustard jar, a milk bottle (if you can get the money back out), or any other container. Of course, if the thief decides to stop in his search to make himself a sandwich and pour a glass of milk, you may be out of luck. If you aren't squeamish, you can also put your folding money in a waterproof container and hide it inside your toilet tank, the square tank behind your bathroom bowl. Other hiding places, such as behind pictures on the wall or inside kitchen canisters, have become so common that the thieves often search them before they consider the usual drawers.

Most people keep their valuables in the master bedroom. The burglar will seek the master bedroom out and usually ignore the children's room except to break into the piggy bank, if he's an unsentimental type. Passing up the piggy bank could be missing a good bet since piggy banks are often better stocked than savings accounts, especially in the past few years. But the thief will gravitate to the master bedroom. Thus when a choice of rooms is available, the master bedroom should be given the most remote location from doors and stairs to make it harder for the thief to reach. If you have a chance to have your master bedroom above the ground floor, by all means do so. The same holds true for the den, which is often a treasure trove containing anything from stamps and coins to guns. If the den is below ground level and far from windows, doors, and other avenues of escape, the thief may be leery of a long stay and pass it by. Wolves and foxes usually build their dens underground. Homeowners who don't want to be robbed should do the same.

When considering a place to hide your most valued possessions, don't overlook the attic. This is the farthest of all rooms from easy access and hence, from easy escape. It may not be cool in summer, or warm in winter—it may look like a burglar has been there already and left a shambles—but the attic is a pretty good bet to be safe from burglars. No burglar wants to get caught in the attic when the whole family comes home for the night. And unless he's an ex-paratrooper homesick for Fort Bragg, he doesn't want to try jumping out a third-floor window either. The only problem with using an attic to store your valuables is that in case of fire you may have access problems yourself. It's up to you to decide which is the greater threat to your property.

ASSESS YOUR VALUABLES

Once inside the house, the thief will open all the doors and ground-floor windows so as to have as many exits as possible in case someone comes to disturb him during his foray. After this, he will rummage around looking for anything valuable, especially if it is small enough to fit into his pocket. Favorite items are cash, jewelry, watches, credit cards, and the like.

The determined thief will head for the master bedroom and conduct a really thorough search, sometimes ripping open mattresses and pillows, tearing out the backs of pictures, and lifting up rugs. Drawers will be ripped out, dumped out, and turned over to look for money taped under the bottoms. Books will be thrown out of their shelves to find out if any of them are hollow. TVs, radios, tape recorders, and guns will probably be stolen. Guns, in fact, are a very hot item on the criminal market. Since stolen guns are very apt to be used in crimes— criminals prefer stolen guns to the registered variety—this is especially crucial to the homeowner. Imagine having to explain why a bullet from a gun registered in your name killed a policeman or a prominent politician.

Make an inventory of anything you own and keep at home that a burglar would steal—money, jewels, credit cards, small appliances, guns, small machine tools, TVs, radios, tape recorders, calculators. Then figure out how much it would cost you to replace all the items you have counted. Remember that prices never remain the same and that unless your appliances are old and decrepit ones, you would probably pay more for them today than you did when you bought them. This total figure would be the cost of a burglary. You don't have to be a rich man to lose thousands of dollars to a burglar. And if you aren't a rich man, you'll have trouble replacing the items you would lose.

Of course, you hope you won't be hit, and if you take the

proper precautions, the odds are against it. But just to make sure, minimize the amount of valuable property you leave lying around. A bank safety deposit box, not a quaint teakwood jewelry chest, is the best place for any really valuable jewelry. If you have expensive cameras, binoculars, and such things that you don't use frequently, and can think of a hiding place that the burglar isn't apt to find—say, a musty old steamer trunk in your attic or basement—by all means keep them there. Guns can be protected by special locks that fit into the trigger guard and can't be removed without damaging the weapon. Anything you can do to make the burglar waste time looking for your goodies is in your favor.

DO-IT-YOURSELF BURGLARY

Now that you've theoretically made all the recommended improvements, it's time for a change of hats. Instead of thinking like a harried homeowner, think like a burglar for a few minutes.

That's right. Pretend that you're a thief trying to plunder your own house.

Go out one evening and drive around your block. Pretend that you're scouting the area. Is your house completely dark, partially lit, or completely illuminated? If it's dark and looks empty, you would try to break in, wouldn't you?

The next step is to walk up to your house and attempt to break in. You can omit the usual first step of ringing the doorbell or pounding on the door to make sure no one is home. Try to pick the lock, as the thief would if he had gotten this far and no one was at home.

If you have a credit card or other strip of plastic, try to slip the card between the door and door frame near the lock. The objective of this probing is to slip the bolt back into the lock, thus unlocking the door. Unless you have a dead bolt lock or unless there is some kind of ridge preventing the insertion of the card into the crack, it's odds-on that even if you can't open the door this way, the burglar probably can. When you open the door—using a key if you're no good at slipping the bolt with the card—look at the lock carefully. If the bolt, which sticks out like a tongue, has a slanted side facing toward the outside of the house, it's a slip bolt lock and a thief probably would be able to make short work of it.

While you're attempting this break-in, keep one eye on the street. If you can see the street, someone on the street can probably see you. Would you feel nervous breaking into the house if you were a burglar? Or would you be confident and secure?

Check around and see if you can find a key for the house anywhere near the front door. Check the usual places—the milkbox, over the doorjamb, the mailbox, under or inside any flowerpots. If you can find the key, rest assured that a thief could find it, too.

Now it's time to check the other doors and windows. Can you get into the house easily through the garage door, simply by breaking a window and reaching in to unlock the door? Is the back door easy to pry open with a card, or is the key lying around someplace convenient? Convenient to you means convenient to the burglar, too. When you stand by your back door, are you in clear view of your neighbor's house, or are you hidden by an awning, trees, or the house itself?

Check the windows to the basement. Do they open at a push, or are they locked tightly or protected by bars? If you can get into the basement, can you enter the main part of the house without dealing with any more locks?

Once you're in the house, look around greedily. Are all the goodies tucked away in unlikely places, or are they lying around waiting to be scooped up and carted off? Is the master bedroom on the same floor and close to the front door, or is it on another floor? If it's on the ground floor, it's that much easier to loot, and that much easier to escape if you're caught.

Now you're done. Don't get carried away and actually steal your own valuables. But ask yourself the question: If I were a burglar, would I find it hard or easy to loot my own home? If your answer is that it's a snap, you'd better get to work making it harder. The next person that breaks into your home may not be you.

4

Security Devices

When the term *security devices* is used nowadays, most people think of a complex array of electronic sensor devices worthy of James Bond—sensors that can x-ray a person from a distance and pick up the telltale Walther PPG pistol under his coat, listening devices implanted in shoes and in potted palm trees, and so forth. Stuff like this is good to have if you're protecting the Hope Diamond or nuclear secrets, and it might even be comforting if you live in certain major cities where there seem to be as many burglars as homeowners. But they don't constitute the whole world of security.

Security devices of one sort or another have been around a long time. In recent years, scientists have discovered that the pyramids, once thought to be obtuse blocks of solid stone, are actually honeycombed with secret passages, some of which were closed off by sliding stones after the pyramids were constructed. The Great Wall of China could also be said to have been a security device of epic proportions, and so was Hadrian's Wall in northern England, built by the Romans to keep out the barbarians. All these security systems, of course, worked for a while, but ultimately they all failed because the people who were using them failed. And, of course, they were all rather expensive.

A good security system doesn't need to take twenty years to build. Some of the best devices are the simplest. For instance, if you worry about somebody pushing in your back door and you pile your empty garbage cans in a heap against the door, this is a security device. And if a thief tries to get in and knocks the cans over, this is a working security device. If you hear the cans fall, or if someone else hears them and phones the police, and if the thief is caught or at least has to flee to escape capture, then you can rate your heap of empty garbage cans a total success as a security device. They may work better than hundreds of more expensive devices which detect the thief but ultimately fail to stop him because nobody is monitoring the system.

Thus, a security device—whether it is the Great Wall of China or a stack of empty garbage cans or a supersophisticated electronic sensor device—is only as good as the human beings who have to respond to it.

In this chapter, we will discuss all sorts of security devices, examine their strong points and weak points, and hopefully give you some insight into which kinds best fit your need.

SIMPLE SECURITY DEVICES

Some time ago in New York City, a woman was justifiably worried about the possibility that burglars might hit her apartment or that muggers or rapists might break in when she was home alone. Every night before she went to bed, she piled up empty tin cans and books against the inside of her front door, and she told the neighbors that if they heard any loud crashes they should call the police and generally raise a ruckus. When a felon did break into her apartment, the cans and books fell with a huge clatter, and all three of her neighbors called the police and set up a racket which frightened the burglar. Through a little time and imagination, the woman was spared a robbery or worse.

Her system, clumsy as it might have looked, was a full-fledged security device, because it aided in the detection of a forcible entry and warned the woman and her friends of the danger.

An equally simple device was used by another New York

woman, a young secretary who worked some distance from her apartment. The building she lived in had a great many senior citizen tenants who spent a good deal of time walking around the halls, visiting back and forth or just stretching their legs. The secretary took advantage of this by slipping a piece of cardboard atop her door when she closed it and asking the oldsters to phone the police if the paper ever disappeared in the daytime when she was at work. The senior citizens, who were glad to be helpful, would give the cardboard a glance each time they walked by. One day, while the young woman was at work, a thief pried her door open and entered the apartment, but in doing so he knocked over the cardboard marker. A passing oldster noticed that the cardboard was gone and toddled on home to call the police. They arrived before the thief was done and caught him at work.

The cardboard was effective in this case, but it had its pitfalls. If the thief had been more observant, he might have seen it drop when he entered and simply replaced it while he plundered the apartment. Similarly, the pile of books was effective only when the New York woman was home. She obviously couldn't pile the books up without remaining inside the apartment. And neither of these devices would have been very effective in a house, because the neighbors wouldn't have been near enough to hear the books and cans fall or to notice the fallen cardboard.

Thus, the security system must be considered in terms of a total environment. If you install a complicated system of claxons and buzzers that ring and wail when someone breaks into your house but nobody hears them and calls the police, the system is useless. With a few rare and illegal exceptions, security systems are not intended to kill or even to repel burglars. They are merely warning devices. The rest is still up to the homeowner or apartment dweller.

DOG SECURITY

Ever since the first shivering wolf cub braved his terror to crawl up next to a caveman's campfire and beg for scraps of meat, man and the dog have been partners in protecting their mutual home from outsiders. The ancient Egyptians mummified their favorite dogs—usually salukis, perhaps the world's oldest purebred dogs—and kept the bodies of their pets in their own tombs so that the dog could go to the afterlife with his master. The ancient Chinese bred huge war dogs, cousins of the modern chow chow, which weighted several hundred pounds. They endowed the dog with all the traits of the warrior hero. In the folk legends of Vietnam, for instance, the Montagnards of the hill country are said to be descendants of the Jade Emperor's daughter and a hero-dog who killed an evil dragon and claimed the princess as his reward. The Emperor had promised the hero-dog half his kingdom, but he weaseled out by giving him the half at the tops of the mountains, which is where the Montagnards live.

American Indians used the dog not only as a hunter and watchdog but as a beast of burden, to pull their sleds and travois. In fact, when horses were first introduced by the white man, the Indians called them "big dogs" or "magic dogs."

Obviously, the dog has been around a long time. Americans in particular have always loved and perhaps sentimentalized their furry friends, and the image of a boy and his dog is one of the fondest evocations of childhood and long summer days. The best known of all sentimental tributes to the dog is that of George Graham Vest, a Missouri lawyer and ex-senator, who was seeking damages from a man who killed his client's dog:

> The one absolutely unselfish friend that a man can have in this selfish world, the one that never deserts him, the one that never proves ungrateful or treacherous, is his dog.
> A man's dog stands by him in prosperity and poverty, in health and in sickness . . . he will kiss the hand that has no food to offer . . . and when the last scene of all comes, and death takes the master in its embrace, and his body is laid away in the cold ground, no matter if all other friends pursue their way, there by the graveside will the noble dog be found, his head between his paws, his eyes sad, but open in alert watchfulness, faithful and true, even in death!

Sounds pretty good, doesn't it? And as far as it goes, it is pretty good. But buyer, beware! When you think about getting a dog to protect your hearth and home, there are a lot of factors to consider.

There's no doubt about it, dogs make excellent security systems in several ways. A dog has a sharper sense of smell and better hearing than a person does, and he may be able to detect a stranger that even the most alert homeowner misses. Dogs who bark noisily and jump around like fleas on a hot brick every time someone comes around the house may be a nuisance to late-sleeping homeowners and a terror to the poor mailman, but they will most definitely discourage the average burglar. Not only will the dog's yapping alert people for a short distance around, but the burglar himself will probably assume that the dog's bite is worse than his bark.

This, however, may be truer than he knows.

Some dogs who habitually try to attack anyone who comes near the house have been known to spring on relatives, friends, salesmen, and children. Contrary to the sentimental pictures drawn by George Graham Vest, a dog makes no distinction between good strangers and bad strangers, and may even attack children if he doesn't know them. A few years ago, a small child in southern New Jersey was torn apart by his family's watchdog.

*A dog is an excellent deterrent to burglary—the bigger the dog, the better the deterrent. Would **you** go into this house? (Courtesy of Mike SanGiovanni.)*

If a dog attacks strangers, unless they are in the act of breaking into your house, you could be liable to charges of *atrocious assault*. This is doubly true if the dog runs loose and attacks some innocent stranger who isn't anywhere near your house. A really vicious dog, or even a bad-tempered and high-strung one, can become a two-edged sword.

The upkeep on a dog is not usually expensive but it is time-consuming. The dog has to be fed at least once a day—more as a puppy—and has to be walked several times a day or given the run of a yard to enable him to evacuate his bowels and to take enough exercise to stay healthy. Dogs have to have periodic shots from a veterinarian not only as a matter of health but, in most places, as a matter of law. Dogs have to be protected against rabies so that they can qualify for licenses. And they have to have licenses every year, in most towns.

Raising a dog from puppyhood has all the pitfalls, but few of the rewards, of bringing up a child. Dogs have to be "toilet trained" in the form of housebreaking, and until they are, you had better be prepared for some disgusting sights and smells around the house. Before a dog drops his milk teeth and grows his adult fangs, he tends to chew on anything that holds still, which will play hob with your furniture. His natural rambunctiousness, especially if he doesn't get much outdoor exercise, may cost you some prized possessions and even some prized friends, if they're afraid of animals. Even after a dog reaches adulthood, he may run off in search of adventure or playmates of the opposite sex on a frequent but unscheduled basis, costing you sleepless nights and possible legal problems.

But that's the bad side of the picture. The good side is that the dog is nature's own burglar alarm, and, incidentally, fire alarm as well. It's a rare burglar who will try to break into a house with a good-sized, aggressive-looking dog visible on the premises. Just living on a block where a lot of people own dogs and walk them at night can be a fringe benefit in your struggle to remain burglarproof.

Once you've decided to get a dog, you still have some secondary decisions to make. Should it be a puppy or a grown dog? A male or female? Pedigreed or a mongrel? Attack-trained or ordinary? A big dog or a little one? All these decisions are important and involve more variables than may be apparent.

The choice between a pup and grown dog revolves largely around whether your needs are strictly security-oriented or emotional. Puppies are cute and cuddly and all that, but they aren't much good for guard duty. In fact, cute as they are, you may find them an unbearable nuisance if you don't have a lot of spare time to take care of them. If you're a serious dog fancier, by all means get a puppy, perhaps a pedigreed one, from a registered kennel or reputable pet shop. But if your needs are security plain and simple and there's no element of snob appeal in your need for a dog, your best bet may be to pick up a stray dog from the pound or from one of the lost pet services. If you shop around, you can sometimes pick up a dog that's housebroken and fully mature for a few dollars, as opposed to $100 or over for a pedigreed dog. There's nothing wrong with a mongrel for security purposes, provided that he fulfills the basic requirement of making noise when somebody comes snooping around.

The ultimate security dog—as well as the ultimate status symbol—is the *attack-trained dog*. These come in two va-

Training a German shepherd as an attack dog involves some hard work and a thick quilted jacket for the trainer. (Courtesy of Emmett François.)

rieties. One type is trained to attack on command. The other type, used in guarding junkyards, guided missile installations, and department stores after closing time, is just plain mean and will attack anybody but his handler. Buying this second type of dog could be a very serious mistake, especially if you have small children. A dog can kill a child in a matter of seconds and inflict grievous injuries even on an adult man, so this type of dog is not recommended for the homeowner.

The attack-trained dog who attacks on command is a little bit safer than the guard dog, but not much safer. You have to be a trained handler to control a dog like this, and they are lethal weapons. Siccing an attack dog is commensurate with shooting somebody, and if you can't prove that your life was in jeopardy when you commanded Rover to kill somebody, you could be charged with atrocious assault or murder. Moreover, the status-symbol value of the attack-trained dog is such that unprofessional kennels and half-baked attack dog services are springing up like mushrooms. Many of the dogs they train are more dangerous to the owner than they are to felons. Attack dogs are also expensive. If you have a sure and certain knowledge that there's somebody roaming around who really wants to kill you (and if you aren't seeing a psychiatrist about this feeling), it might be worth the trouble to get one, but for the average citizen, attack dogs are a needless and dangerous luxury.

If you decide that you can't live without an attack dog, you should ask the trainer or dog service one question: Is the dog the right age? It's a serious mistake to attack-train a dog before he's at least a year and a half to two years old. Training him as an attack dog involves brutalizing him to some extent, and if the dog is exposed to too much hostility at too young an age, he may become neurotic, irritable, and erratic—just as a young human being may become unfeeling or demented because of an excessively brutal childhood. Again, this is a good argument against an attack dog. If the dog can't be ready for sale until he's three or four, he's probably only got six or seven useful years left. Some dogs may live to be fifteen or even twenty, but ten to twelve is the average life span. Most attack dogs are either German shepherds or Doberman pinschers. You should choose between the two breeds. Until recently, shepherds had the reputation of being more reliable, but so many shepherds have been bred recently to fill the need for attack dogs and other home guards that some experts feel the breed is in decline. Dobermans have a bad name for viciousness, but this is probably exaggerated. Before the dog craze began, the Doberman was generally used for jobs that required attack, while the shepherds were used for tasks that required intelligence as well as courage and vicious strength. Either dog, when trained, is a lethal adversary—perhaps as much because of the panic they evoke as by their actual power. If you just want a dog to scare people, without being attack-trained, a Doberman or a German shepherd will do the job nicely. There's something about the sight of a Doberman that is apt to turn the toughest crook's blood to ice water.

The problem of a big dog versus a little dog is largely one of how much space you have and how much you want to pay for food. A big dog, obviously, is a lot more frightening to an intruder. Big dogs, very generally, also have better dispositions than small dogs. But a big dog needs space to run around and get exercise. If you have an enclosed yard, or can build

Attack dogs can be terrifying to innocent bystanders as well as to criminals. (Courtesy of Emmett François.)

one, then a big dog is your best bet. But if you live in a two-room apartment, then you'll have to compromise on a small dog that can get by without a big exercise area. A little dog also eats less, which is more significant than you might think if you've never owned a big dog. If you have a big dog and he eats prime canned food, it can cost you $5 a week and up to feed him.

The decision between a male and a female dog is partly a matter of price, since female dogs are usually cheaper. Male dogs are less trouble—they never go into heat or get pregnant, and they usually have a more even temper. Female dogs can become pregnant if they get out of the house, and this leads to the problem of puppies.

Granted, puppies are fluffy and cute and adorable. The fact remains that as the country becomes urbanized there are just too many dogs running around, and you're probably going to have a devil of a time giving away puppies. *Don't*, above all, think that you can have a handy side income through dog breeding. Unless you plan to become an expert and devote half your life to caring for dogs, you'll probably lose money, not to mention sleep, by trying to breed dogs commercially. If you have the female dog spayed, that is, sterilized, you won't have to worry about puppies, but spaying may affect the dog's disposition.

Now you know the best and the worst. Dogs can be a nuisance, and if you don't like animals or are extremely fastidious or allergic to hair, it may be better to pass one up. But if you can form a working partnership with a dog, you'll have one of the best of all burglar alarms working full-time to protect your home, and a deterrent whose very appearance will discourage nine out of ten prowlers.

GUN SECURITY

Whenever a wave of burglaries or muggings sweeps over a community, homeowners flock to their local sporting goods stores to buy guns or rush to the police station to fill out gun permits.

The reaction isn't surprising. In fact, it's quite understandable, since the gun has been one of the principal tools of

American civilization. The childhood heroes that most people grew up with, whether they were Daniel Boone, Davy Crockett, Wyatt Earp, or Hopalong Cassidy, real or fictional, were all gunmen *par excellence*. And eighty or a hundred years ago, a great many American men carried guns, in the city as well as on the frontier. In some Western and Southern states, guns are still extremely common. This is all part of the American scene.

Unfortunately, the result of all this boyhood nostalgia has been to convince every peaceable suburbanite that he need only strap on a Colt .45 to turn into Matt Dillon. This is tragically untrue. A great many people, perhaps most people, have no real knowledge of guns and no business owning them, carrying them, or playing with them. Most statistical breakdowns indicate that the homeowner who tries to use a gun to stop a burglary is more likely to shoot himself or a relative than he is to shoot a burglar. Guns are said to account for five times as many shootings against family and friends as they are against prowlers, though not all of this carnage is the result of bungled attempts at playing Wyatt Earp. Many of these injuries and fatalities undoubtedly result from quarrels, drunken or otherwise, or the tragic curiosity of children.

The major factor in buying a gun, then, is deciding whether the burglar or the gun poses the greatest threat to life and property—especially life. If your family life is happy and stable, and if you don't have any curious children, moody teenagers, or violent drunks in the family, then a gun may—just may—be a worthwhile security investment. But if you have a single unstable person in the house, keeping a gun around is like smoking in bed—over a powder keg.

Once having made the decision to buy the gun, you must consider several factors. Do you want to buy a long arm or a handgun? What caliber? What type of action? Where will you keep it?

There are two basic types of firearm within the reach and needs of the ordinary citizen: *long arms*, meaning rifles and shotguns, and *handguns*. Long arms have several advantages and several disadvantages. For one thing, long arms are usually easier to purchase. Several bills now being discussed call for a total or partial ban on civilian ownership of handguns, but only the most extreme legislators would dare suggest that

Americans give up their rifles and shotguns. There are two reasons for this. Rifles and shotguns have a clear purpose over and above man-to-man shooting, since they are used for hunting. And rifles and shotguns are seldom used in robberies because they are too long and too heavy to be conveniently concealed.

Long arms are easier to use accurately than handguns. Every red-blooded American male may consider himself Wyatt Earp, but army ordnance officers know better. During World War II, the army rushed the M-2 carbine (a small rifle) into mass production because the military wanted a long arm for troops who didn't engage in combat as a primary mission and would normally have carried pistols. However, such a minority of soldiers really understood how to use a pistol properly that most men did more damage to themselves and one another than to the enemy.

Long arms have one great disadvantage in home protection: They are so long that it is inconvenient to keep them close enough to you to do any good in the event of a sudden break-in, and you may even have trouble swinging a long-barreled rifle or shotgun into play in cramped quarters. Moreover, the average hunting or military rifle is designed for shooting your fellowman at ranges up to a mile away. If you shoot at a burglar inside and miss, or even if you hit him, the bullet may keep traveling and kill somebody in the next apartment or outside the house. The power of even the crudest modern military rifle is awesome and not to be trifled with. Too many Westerns and war movies have popularized the image of the firearm as a 4th of July noisemaker that you can bang away with all day with no regard to consequences. This is a criminal attitude and has led to the deaths of a good many innocent people who were hit by bullets from guns they never even heard or saw, because some dumb-dumb thought he could fire off a military rifle as if it were a .22 or a cap pistol.

Unless you live on a farm somewhere out in the north woods and expect an imminent visit from the Manson family, a military rifle isn't suited to your safety needs. A shotgun may be a slightly better bet. For the benefit of the uninitiated, a shotgun is a long arm that looks rather like a rifle. But instead of firing a solid bullet for long distances, it usually fires a scattered charge of small bullets, called "pellets" or "shot," for short distances. The charge spreads out after it leaves the barrel and covers a lot of space. Shotguns are intended for use against small moving targets—flying birds, rabbits, and so forth. At close range they can inflict terrible and lethal wounds on people, burglars or otherwise. Police often use shotguns in close combat, where it is vital to knock down their assailants with a single shot and where they may not have time to aim accurately. Shotguns account for a slightly larger proportion of gunshot fatalities than rifles. Robbers sometimes saw the *stock* (the wooden back end) and the *barrel* off a shotgun and use it in holdups. A *sawed-off shotgun* inflicts hideous wounds, and getting shot with one, even if you live, is a lot worse than getting shot with a rifle. But they don't present the same danger to an innocent pedestrian walking a half-mile away that a rifle does, and if you want a long arm for home protection, a shotgun is a better bet.

Handguns are the most popular type of weapon purchased purely for home defense, and cause by far the greatest number of fatalities, to innocent and guilty alike. They also figure in a far larger number of crimes than long arms do.

There are two basic types of modern handguns: the *revolver* and the *automatic pistol*. The revolver is the kind of weapon, more or less, that Wyatt Earp and Matt Dillon use on TV. In its

The breech of an expensive shotgun, showing a gun lock to prevent anyone but the owner from using the gun, and to discourage theft. It is almost impossible to remove the lock without ruining the gun. (Courtesy of Master Lock Co.)

present form it is an American invention. Sam Colt, the inventor of the modern revolver, is said to have gotten the idea for his revolver while he was a seaman watching the ship's wheel go around in a circle. He devised a cylindrical metal chamber which held five or six charges of powder and lead and which turned around a spindle rod until each chamber rested against the rear of the gun's single barrel. By legend, at least, the Colt revolver enabled the Texas Rangers to gain the advantage over the Comanche Indians, who had previously given them a good beating using bows and arrows against the Texans' single-shot guns. Revolvers came into their own during the Civil War and for many years were the only type of handgun in popular use. Around the turn of the century, the automatic pistol, perfected in Europe, first became popular. Instead of holding its bullets in a cylinder, the automatic carries them in a flat *magazine*, or clip, that usually slips into the butt of the gun.

Revolvers come in two types—*single action*, in which the

A modern Colt revolver, with gun lock. Most police forces prefer revolvers, while most armies use automatics. (Courtesy of Master Lock Co.)

shooter has to cock the hammer of the gun back before each shot, and *double action*, in which he merely pulls the trigger and the revolver fires each time the trigger is pulled. A revolver usually holds six shots in its cylinder. An automatic usually has seven shots in its magazine, but may have as many as twelve.

Shooters differ as to the merits of the revolver and the automatic. Many gun experts claim that the revolver is more reliable and that automatics have a tendency to jam—that is, not to fire—especially when they aren't cleaned regularly. Revolvers are usually bulkier than automatics. If it matters, most police departments use revolvers, while most armies use automatics. If you decide to buy a handgun at all, the choice between a revolver and an automatic is one that will confront you. Price differences are usually more a matter of workmanship than of type, so firing action of the weapon is the main factor.

Caliber is also important. A caliber, in the sense we refer to here, is 1/100 inch. In the English-speaking world, the size of the bullet a gun shoots is usually given in calibers. The smallest popular caliber is .22, which means that the bore of the gun is less than 1/4 inch. The largest popular handgun caliber is

Representative cartridges: Left to right, a 7.62 mm rifle cartridge, a .357 magnum, a .38 special wadcutter (target bullet), a .22 long rifle, and a .22 short cartridge. Size indicates people should think twice before buying a heavy-caliber firearm, because the kick may be too much for them. (Courtesy of Mike SanGiovanni.)

.45, or a little bit under half an inch. Handguns also come in .25, .32, and .38 caliber. Two other types of handgun are the .357 and .44 magnum calibers. These are extra-powerful guns whose cartridges contain a heavier proportion of explosive than ordinary cartridges. European guns are sometimes 7 or 9 millimeters. A millimeter is 1/1000 meter.

The .22, the lightest handgun (or rifle) caliber, is popular because ammunition is cheap and thus is a favorite size for target shooters. Unfortunately, if you ever have to take on a burly burglar and come to the point of shooting him, you may find that he can absorb a lot of lead from a .22 before he goes down. A single shot can be fatal, but then again it is quite possible to hit an assailant two or three times with a .22 without killing him—or even without stopping a vicious attack until the victim is dead himself. When the United States Army was fighting the Moro tribesmen in the Philippines around 1900, they found that even the .38 cartridge wasn't powerful enough for their purposes. The Moros, who got themselves high on drugs and the Koran, could be shot several times with a .38 and still live long enough to behead the unhappy troopers with their bolo knives, though they might have died of shock and blood loss afterwards. The army had to reintroduce the old .45 caliber pistol cartridge from the Indian wars to be sure of killing or disabling an opponent with a single shot. They did this by designing a new pistol, the .45 automatic, which is still in use. A .45 will stop just about anything and inflicts utterly hideous wounds. The hole where the bullet enters the body may be a neat puncture, but the exit wound is as big as a fist.

The negative factor about any of the big guns—other than the uselessness of an apology if you make a mistake—is their recoil. When a gun is fired, the bullet is pushed out the front end, and the back of the gun is pushed against your hand or shoulder in reaction.

With a small-caliber weapon, like a .22, this recoil is barely perceptible. But with a big gun, like a .45 or .357 magnum, the recoil may be heavy enough to be really unpleasant for a woman or even for a small man. The gun may seem to want to jump out of your hand. In fact, it may just do that, which can be embarrassing, especially if it goes off a second time when it hits the floor and takes part of your head off.

The best plan is this: If you seriously want to buy a gun, and can cope with the hazards, go to a shooting range which rents guns for target practice. Ask the owner or manager to show you a few guns and try them out on the target range, with him or some other experienced shooter acting as an instructor. When you find one that you feel comfortable with and you can afford, that's the gun for you. If you find that you hate all guns when you try them out, so much the better.

Once you decide to buy a gun, you'll realize what you're getting yourself into. In many states, you have to get a permit from the local police station, signed by the chief. Sometimes, too, you will be fingerprinted and the fingerprints sent to the FBI to find out if you have a criminal record. You may also be asked to sign a statement attesting that you have never been confined for mental illness, addicted to drugs, and so forth. Sometimes you will also have to provide character witnesses. This seems like a nuisance, but a gun is a deadly weapon, and it's logical that it should at least be as difficult to buy a gun as it is to get a driver's license.

Unfortunately, only a few states or communities require the potential gun owner to pass a test indicating proficiency with a gun, as he or she would when taking out a driver's license. If you're of good character, you can buy a gun without even knowing how to load it in virtually any state in the union. In some states, mostly in the South or West, you don't need a permit to purchase a gun. You can walk into any sporting goods store and buy a lethal weapon as easily as if you were buying a hammer or saw.

Whether it is easy or hard to buy a gun in your state or hometown, there are certain standards that should be observed at all times when dealing with guns. These are, briefly:

1. *Always* assume that any gun you see is loaded. Even if it's your own gun and you remember unloading it, don't overlook the possibility that your memory could have played you false or that somebody else loaded it. Always check a gun carefully to find out if it is loaded before handling it further.

A safety lock is a must for a gun owner, to prevent family tragedies as well as theft. (Courtesy of Master Lock Co.)

Never point it at anyone else or any part of your own body while doing so.

2. *Never* point a gun at anything you don't intend to kill, even when the gun is unloaded. You could have overlooked a shell lodged in the firing chamber, and you could be responsible for killing or crippling a friend, a stranger, or yourself.

3. *Never* leave a gun, loaded or unloaded, anywhere where children or other strangers can get their hands on it. Children see so many Westerns and cartoons that they assume any gun is as harmless as a cap pistol. Even if the gun is empty and no bullets are around, a playmate may offer to get bullets from somewhere else.

4. When carrying a gun, loaded or unloaded, don't cock it. Leave the safety catch, if there is one, locked, and always keep it pointed at the ground. Thus if the gun goes off through your clumsiness, the bullet will go into the ground harmlessly, and not flying off to kill somebody half a mile away.

5. *Never* store a gun where it will be exposed to intense

heat or moisture. Extreme heat may cause the cartridges to detonate. Moisture may make the gun rust and render it inoperative.

6. Buy one of the trigger-guard safety locks sold in better sporting goods stores and lock up your gun. These locks slip over the trigger guard, the metal ring protecting the trigger, and they cannot be removed by children, or frequently, by anyone else without damaging the gun.

The decision to buy a gun is a tough one and should entail a good deal of soul-searching. On the one hand, the gun owner may face the type of situation that confronted an Illinois homeowner. He thought he heard a prowler, seized the loaded pistol from his night table, and fired a shot at a shadowy figure. He learned as he turned on the lights he had killed his teenaged daughter.

On the other hand, what would have been the effect on the Manson family killers if even one of their five victims had been able to produce a gun? Would five, or perhaps far more than five, lives have been saved by armed self-defense? In the final analysis, the question of gun ownership has to be decided on an individual basis, by every individual person.

LOCKS

Locks, at least, are incontrovertible. Unlike dogs or guns, they have no emotional detractors. Anyone who doesn't lock his doors, anywhere in these United States, is either a saintly ascetic or a damned fool.

The very mention of doors without locks is a harbinger of all sorts of nostalgia, if not of fantasy and ancient history. The Spanish conquistadores were astounded to see the highly civilized Indians of Peru walk out of their homes and merely prop a stick against the door as a sign that no one was home. Even at this early date, in the 1500s, no civilized urban European would have been that foolhardy. And since then, needless to say, things have gotten a lot worse. Those old Irish ballads which mention "the ould door without any key" are probably more an honest comment on rural Irish poverty and the absence of anything worth stealing than they are on the hopelessly quaint notion, even then, that one's neighbors were all honest. Locks have been around since the days of pharaohs, and today they are absolutely necessary.

The only controversy that can possibly arise is to the type of lock one should have, and even here the answer is concrete! Get a dead bolt lock, as soon as possible, for every important door on your house.

When you go into a locksmith's shop and see the various types and brand names of locks available, you will probably be overwhelmed by the vast array on sale. But don't let yourself be led astray. There are only three types of locks—slip bolt, *reverse slip bolt*, and dead bolt.

Each lock, of whatever type, has three major parts: the *cylinder*, which contains the keyhole, the *cylinder housing*, which supports the cylinder, and the *bolt*, the metal rod that extends out of the lock and into the door frame to make the door fast. The bolt, of course, is activated by twisting a key in the keyhole, either opening or locking the door. There are other parts inside the lock—springs, tumblers, and so forth—but the three main parts remain the same in all mechanical locks.

The *tumblers*, which are inside the lock and not visible, are the working parts that respond to the key. Different combinations or patterns of tumblers ensure that the same key won't open every lock. What a windfall for a burglar it would be to find the universal key to all locks! Fortunately for homeowners and their peace of mind, no such universal key exists. Although it is possible to pick virtually any lock and line up the tumblers, the average burglar is not a lockpicker and neither has the time nor the skill necessary. If the front of your house is well lighted, he won't want to pause there long enough to work on a lock, so you're safe from all but the most daring and determined crooks.

It is just because the average thief is not a cracksman, or lockpick, that the dead bolt lock is so important; you don't need to be a lockpicker to open a house protected only by the slip bolt lock.

A slip bolt lock: The bolt face slants away from the outside (to the right). Slip bolt locks are easily picked. (Courtesy of Mike SanGiovanni.)

To find out just what kind of lock you do have, go to your door and stand outside. Find the lock and activate it so the bolt is extended, like a naughty boy's tongue sticking out. If the face of the bolt has a slant to it, like a wedge, and the slant faces outside, toward the street, you have a slip bolt lock. And you're in big trouble.

Run your finger gently up against the lock. Notice how the bolt slides back into the door? Well, a burglar can do the same thing with a celluloid card or a special tool and have your house open to inspection and plunder in a matter of seconds.

If the slant on the lock faces inside, toward your living space, then you have a reverse slip bolt lock. This is trickier to open than the regular slip bolt, but it would still be relatively easy for a dedicated burglar to get inside. Your best bet is to insist on a dead bolt lock.

After you've insisted on a dead bolt lock, consider the type of cylinder before making a purchase. Basically, there are two types of cylinders: the one that fits onto the surface of the

The 3M Lock Alarm features a dead bolt lock and chain coupled to a highly sensitive battery-powered solid state electronic alarm. It provides pre-entry protection because any attempt to force the lock, dead bolt, chain, or door itself sets off a shrill, pulsating signal before entry is gained. (Courtesy of 3M Co.)

door, and one that has a keyhole in the doorknob. The better cylinder is the one on the door proper. A thief who isn't afraid to make a little noise can smash the doorknob right off the door, and the doorknob cylinder with it, and then open the door with comparative ease. Breaking the knob off will sometimes even directly expose the tumblers or the bolt, which makes it easy to open the door.

When the cylinder is seated firmly inside the door, the burglar would have to tear the whole door apart to open the lock, and he would be unlikely to take this risk in a crowded residential area unless he were uncommonly eager to get inside your house. The process would prove extremely noisy as well as time-consuming.

Another type of lock, recently developed, is opened by combination, and instead of having to use a key, you merely dial three to six numbers and the lock opens. This is very sophisticated, but it has its pitfalls. True, with this kind of lock, you won't be inconvenienced by forgetting the key. But if you forget the combination, you're *really* in trouble. People who still nurture traumatic memories of being late for homeroom in high school because they couldn't get their school lockers open will probably be dead set against this kind of lock from the outset. One solution to the problem of combinations is to match the combination with the numbers of your phone number. Unfortunately, this clever device may backfire if the thief has cased your house well enough to know your phone number.

At any rate, the problem of forgetting your keys won't happen if you own a dead bolt lock because the dead bolt requires you to turn the lock by key whenever you go in *or* out. This may seem inconvenient, but it's not nearly as inconvenient as being robbed or worse because somebody picked your lock with a credit card. Neither the slip bolt lock nor the reverse slip bolt requires the use of a key to lock, but neither of them is as safe as a dead bolt lock.

When you've decided to get a dead bolt lock, your best course is to go to a reputable locksmith and have him install one for you. This may cost somewhat more than if you do the job yourself, but there are pitfalls to installing your own lock, unless you're a skilled amateur carpenter. For one thing, if you don't have the tools required, you'll have to go out and buy them, which will probably cost more than the cost of having a locksmith put the lock in. For another, if you fudge up the job and damage your door, you'll have to buy a new door and have it hung, which may cost upwards of $100. Should the locksmith foul up, he'll almost certainly be covered by insurance and will make restitution for free.

If you intend to install your own lock, make sure that you follow the instructions slowly and carefully. One slip can cost you a door.

If you decide to hire a locksmith to do the work, make sure that the one you select is reputable. As with any other profession, the locksmith's trade has its share of people who are dishonest or just plain sloppy as well as its competent professionals. The local Better Business Bureau can probably provide a list of the locksmiths in any given area and descriptions of complaints against any who are known to be incompetent or dishonest. In some cases, they may have lists ready for requests. In other cases, you may have to select the name out of the phone book's yellow pages and then send it to them.

Another method, which may be somewhat more time-consuming, is to write to the lock manufacturer and ask for the names of reputable locksmiths in your area. The manufacturers are preoccupied with building and maintaining a reputation for integrity and will probably recommend only the best tradesmen.

Once you have the names of several locksmiths, check their rates and compare. Estimates may range anywhere from $10 to $50 or more, so don't be embarrassed to do a little comparison shopping. It will take longer to install a lock in an older, solid-wooden door than in a modern, hollow-core door.

While thinking about a lock, you should also consider a

Above: This lock opens when the homeowner presses four buttons in the proper sequence. Right: Another push-button combination lock. (Courtesy of Presto-Matic Lock Company.)

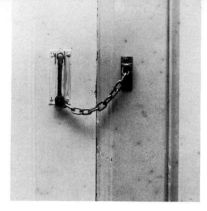

A badly hung door chain. The slide is set vertically instead of horizontally. (Courtesy of Mike SanGiovanni.)

chain to increase security. The main use of a chain is to hold the door half-closed when you look outside in response to a ring or knock at the door. The chain also is used for additional security when you are at home. A burglar may be able to slip your lock, especially if it is a slip bolt, but he may then be foiled by the chain.

The chain, however, is not totally reliable. Most of the chains sold in hardware stores don't have long enough screws holding them in place and can be kicked in by anyone who weighs over 100 pounds. They can also be sawed through, if the thief is able to pick the main lock, or cut with a bolt cutter. At best they provide a small measure of added security, and since they are cheap and easy to set up, they may be worth the price.

When setting up a chain, make sure you install it properly. The *latch-piece*, which accepts the chain, should be higher than the *chain retainer*, and the chain should be loose enough so that the door can be opened a bit, but tight enough so that a hand can't reach in and unlatch the chain. Also, the screws used should be long enough to get a good deep purchase in the wood of the door and the door frame. If they aren't, buy longer screws of the right diameter and substitute them. You may never be able to put up a door chain that will stop a lineman from the Chicago Bears, but you should at least have one strong enough to make an attempted break and entry noisy and arduous.

A better device than a chain, especially for the woman or older person who lives alone, is one of the peephole devices that can be installed in doors. These devices, usually in the form of a brass tube about as thick as a small pen and only a few inches long, use lenses to afford a wide angle view of what's going on outside your door. They can be installed simply by boring a hole through the door with a large standard-sized drill bit, and then screwing the apparatus together like a nut and bolt. Once installed, this viewer allows you to survey the outside of your front door and identify anyone who rings your doorbell.

ELECTRONIC SECURITY

The electronic revolution has undoubtedly been the biggest technological breakthrough of the second half of the twentieth century, and the progress that science has made in electronics has reshaped the world to the same degree that gunpowder, the internal-combustion engine, and manned flight have changed our lives. Television, stereophonic sound, and all sorts of sophisticated radio equipment are the portion of the

A door chain, properly hung, and a peephole in an apartment door. The lock in the knob, however, is a bad idea since breaking off the knob makes the lock useless. (Courtesy of Mike SanGiovanni.)

electronic age most visible to the average consumer, but other facets are more startling. The increased use of electronic guidance systems for missiles, of portable battlefield radar sets, and of tiny sensor devices no bigger than a nickel make the pre-1941 army seem as anachronistic as General Sherman's men marching through Georgia. Newspaper comic strip readers of the 1930s dismissed Dick Tracy's portable wrist radio as a piece of improbable science fiction, yet today, far tinier and more powerful radio transmitters are used for everything from phony magic acts to the tapping of gangster's bathrooms.

It may be surprising, with all the technology pioneered for warfare and later developed for leisure, that more hasn't been done to provide electronic weapons for the war against crime. In fact, there are a number of electronic devices available for security purposes to anyone who can afford them. The reason that these devices haven't made more of an impact is that most people don't place the same value on security that they do on entertainment.

Despite the gadgetry available for electronic security, the same caveat exists with electronic surveillance as with the more crude devices people rig up from tin cans, books, and pieces of cardboard. If there is no one around to respond to the warning signal, it won't do any good.

Most electronic security devices consist of two parts: the *sensor* and the *alarm*. The sensor picks up the vibrations that indicate a person is in a given region through electronic detection of a change in light or sound or pressure. The alarm, it is hoped, alerts the homeowner, neighbors, or police in time to catch or frighten the prowler.

Sensors work like switches. When a person's presence completes—or perhaps breaks—a circuit, they trigger an alarm. A very simple example would be two metal strips on a door and door frame, touching one another and carrying a low electrical charge. When the strips are disconnected (by opening the door), the circuit is broken and the alarm is discharged.

This is a simple but essentially accurate description of one type of burglar alarm, the type frequently attached to win-

*Door Devices—Electrical tape, which appears to be decorative
design from outside, leads to cables on inside. If glass is broken or
door opened without deactivating system with special key, the
alarm sounds. (Courtesy of Joseph Giardelli.)*

dows to sound if they are pried open without disconnecting
the alarm. The Achilles' heel of this system is that unless you
are home, or your neighbors call the police, the buzzing of a
few claxons probably won't do much to catch a thief, though it
may very well scare him off. Another pitfall is that if the alarm
system works by house current and the thief sees the alarm
and still wants to enter, he can simply cut the power line to
your house and plunder it at leisure, without touching off the
alarm. Some alarms of this type, however, work by self-
contained batteries, and this presents a more serious problem
to the would-be thief.

To adequately protect a house with electronic devices, every
point of entry on the first floor should be covered: doors,
windows, crawl spaces if they lead to the living spaces.
Whether or not you want to invest in electronic devices de-
pends largely on your own volition and on the conditions
you're facing. If you have a lot of valuable property at home,
and if burglaries are frequent in your area, you probably
should go electronic. If your home and possessions are modest

and you live in a low-burglary area, if you're home most of the time and own a large dog, it may be a waste of money.

Once you've decided to go electronic, there is an array of equipment available. One type often used in industrial or retail establishments is the *ultrasonic sensor*. These devices send out a high-pitched sound wave and receive the same sound. They are inaudible to normal human ears, though a dog, or a person with ultrasharp hearing, may pick out a faint sound from the ultrasonic system. When an unexpected sound disrupts the sound waves of the ultrasonic alarm system, the sensors trip an alarm device.

These devices, when used to protect a home, are set up to cover areas where the burglar would have to pass to enter the most important parts of the house. To protect the living room, if it is a large one, two sensor-receivers might be set up, each covering an area of 20 or 30 feet. The homeowner would simply turn on the system when leaving the home. Any noise would then disturb the sensors and trigger an alarm. The sensor devices are often disguised as common household objects—a hi-fi speaker, for instance—so the thief who blunders into an ultrasonic surveillance area might not know he was detected until police, tipped off by an alarm touched off at the station house, arrived on the scene.

There are pitfalls to the sonic detector. It isn't one of those magical devices that supposedly has a brain of its own; on the contrary, it is utterly brainless, and will respond to a noise from you, or your dog or cat, in the same way that it would to an armed prowler. In other words, if you yourself forget to detach the device when you return home, or if your dog goes on a barking spree while you're away, the alarm will trip just as if a prowler had broken in. Sensors set up in schools often bring the police flocking to investigate when some passing punk lofts a rock through the window—the noise of the breaking glass is enough to touch off the device.

The best use for an ultrasonic detector is protecting a certain specific area—a hallway that has to be passed to reach the master bedroom, for instance, or for the master bedroom itself or the den, if you have valuables there. Sensors disguised as books or other commonplace things are available for this sort of protection.

Another common electronic device is the electric eye, which made quite a media flash in the 1950s. The electric eye is often used to count people entering buildings (supermarkets, for instance) and also watches the doors of closed shops after hours. Basically, the electric eye is a sensor that picks up light which is beamed to it. When the beam of light is cut off, the sensor triggers a response.

The system is not new. Militarily, the electric eye principle was first used during World War II, when flights of rockets were launched at airplanes attacking naval convoys. The idea was that the electric eye would trigger an explosive charge in the rocket when the plane's shadow cut off its sunlight. Unfortunately, the rocketeers found out that the rockets were also touched off by the shadows of seagulls and clouds, and that

Disguised as an **English Language Dictionary,** *the new Book Intruder Alarm uses high-frequency sound waves to detect intruders and scare them away with a built-in siren. (Courtesy of 3M Co.)*

Providing protection for vulnerable patio doors and windows, 3M Patio Door Lock Alarm is battery-powered and emits a loud, warning siren if attempt is made to force entry. (Courtesy of 3M Co.)

using them at all in cloudy weather was a hazard. Today, improved versions are used by many nations in anti-aircraft missiles. The pitfall of using the electric eye as a burglar alarm is the same as it was for using it to touch off rockets—just as it can't tell a plane from a seagull, it can't tell a cat from a burglar.

The electric eye sensor unit comes in two parts. One part is the source of light and the other is a reflector to send the beam of light back to be received by the sensor. This beam of light points up another weakness of the electric eye system. The beam of light is clearly visible to the burglar in a dark room, and he may see it and simply duck under the beam or otherwise avoid breaking the circuit and triggering the alarm. For this reason, the light-beam type of detector is generally less efficient than the sound detector. While it may have its uses, it should not be employed without the use of other security devices, though its very appearance may help intimidate an irresolute burglar.

Another type of electronic sensor works by pressure. These

come in all sizes and shapes, and the principle involved is rather like that of the land mines used so extensively in World War II or the booby traps of the Vietnam conflict. If the pressure sensor is stepped on, or possibly dislodged, it will send out a signal that can either trip an alarm or notify the police.

The type of sensor that a person steps on to trigger is referred to, quite logically, as a *step-on sensor*. The type which is tripped when an object is lifted or dislodged is called a *step-off sensor*. The step-on sensors are best placed under rugs at critical places—at the front and back doors, and on the way to the master bedroom, the den, or wherever else valuables are stored. The step-off sensor is best used for protection of a specific object—a valuable painting, for instance. If anyone lifts the painting, it triggers the alarm.

Another type of sensor is specifically designed to protect folding money left in a drawer. Shaped like a money clip, the sensor fits onto the money, and if a thief tries to open the clip, the sensor is activated, and an alarm is tripped.

The cheapest kinds of sensors, yet perhaps the most effective, are those which simply fit against windows and trip off if the windows are pried open. These can be fitted to every ground-floor window in the house, to doors, and to other possible avenues of forcible entry.

Most types of sensor can be purchased from a major locksmith or security specialist. The buyer, however, and not the hired expert, should determine exactly what kind of security he wants and how much he is willing to pay. Remember that even the most complicated and expensive system can be deactivated by turning off the house electricity unless the system is powered by an independent generator.

ALARMS

The best sensor system in the world is useless without a good alarm system to summon help once the thief is detected. Thus the alarm, in a way, is even more important than the sensor.

The *bell alarm*, one of the most common types, is just that—a large bell which rings when a sensor is touched off. These alarms are often used in commercial establishments, as well as some private homes. The problem is that if no one is around to hear the alarm ringing, the thief, if his nerves are cool, can plunder at his leisure. Especially in commercial areas, which are often empty at night, the sound of the bell may be over-looked for a long time unless a police patrol happens to pass by at the crucial moment. The same is true of other sound alarms, which differ only in that they employ a siren or a buzzer instead of a bell.

Sound alarms are also usually vulnerable to the simple ploy of cutting off the electricity. Cutting a single wire, in some cases, can immobilize the whole system.

Another pitfall is the location of the system. Usually the bell alarm or buzzer is located outside the building. If the noisemaker is situated out of the burglar's reach, all he has to do is remove it, and the whole system is useless. Some com-panies have placed "pick-proof" boxes around the bell or buzzer, but the thieves eluded this blockade by shooting two or three cans of shaving cream into the box, which muffles the sound of the bell to a gentle clatter.

A better type of alarm system exists. Some sensors trip a device which will call a preprogrammed telephone number and play a tape recorded voice announcing that a burglary is

This master box controls all the electronic sensors in a house system: if the box is deactivated, the whole system fails. (Courtesy of Joseph Giardelli.)

in progress and giving the address. The preprogrammed device may be the phone number of the police or a licensed guard service, or sometimes of a neighbor, and the device usually makes the call without the knowledge of the thief.

A variation of this alarm system is called the *silent alarm system*. When the sensors detect a break-in, they trigger an alarm system which operates a flashing light at the desk of the police station. The police dispatcher has only to direct a car or cars to the house being entered and the burglar will have a very unpleasant surprise when he tries to leave. Without a doubt, this is the best type of alarm to have, since instead of merely frightening the thief away, it should take him out of circulation for a while and, by example, dissuades others from taking up crime as a vocation.

The service has its drawbacks. It is expensive, and not all police departments encourage, or even permit, the use of their station as a terminal for the silent alarm system. Some allow commercial buildings to use the silent alarm system, but decline to let homeowners set up connections. Since the device works over telephone lines, the monthly phone bill will climb a bit when you use a silent system. And, again because of telephone lines, the silent alarm system is vulnerable to being immobilized if the lines are cut by the burglar or knocked down in bad weather.

If the local police won't cooperate with a silent alarm hookup, it will be a lot cheaper to install one of the automatic dialing systems instead. Hooking a silent alarm into a security service is not cheap, and unless the security service has an office nearby it may be an exercise in futility. Being connected to a service where the agents have to drive 20 miles to answer an alarm isn't going to catch many burglars.

Last but not least, there is the use of psychology to provide security. This involves exploiting the housebreaker's own fear as a weapon to deter him from entering your home.

If you yourself were to approach a door at a factory or public building and saw a sign that said "Do Not Enter" or "Off Limits," you might very well be deterred from entering. If you did enter, you might be fearful or nervous, since previous experience had taught you that signs were supposed to be obeyed. You would have the same attitude that a motorist should ideally have toward a red traffic light or a stop sign. The hardened burglar, whether amateur or professional, is not apt to be frightened off by a sign that says "Do Not Enter." He knows that he is breaking the law by entering your house in any case. You can deter him, however, by playing on the things he does fear.

Nine out of ten burglars prefer not to enter a house that is occupied and to avoid confronting homeowners, both because of the danger of being caught or recognized or injured and because they know they may become involved in much more serious charges than burglary if they get into an altercation. Thus if the owner leaves the radio or the television turned on at its normal volume when he goes out, and the burglar hears the noise from outside, he will probably assume that someone is home and keep away.

A more sophisticated version of this standard trick would be to tape-record some commonplace household sounds and have the recording ready to replay for the burglar's benefit when a sensor triggers the tape recorder. Sounds of people talking and moving around, noises of a dog barking, and other household noises may help convince the thief to beat a fast retreat. One homeowner recorded sounds as if he had just been awakened from a nap. When a thief pried his way into the house and tripped a sensor, the tape recorder began to play a recording of the man shouting, "What the hell was that!" The thief left hurriedly.

Another method is to link up the bedroom or living room lights with the sensor so that when the thief enters, the lights switch on. This gives the impression that his entry has been overheard and will probably cause him to panic.

Warning signs, if they seem reasonable, are also a good psychological deterrent. "Beware of the Dog" is a standby, even if you don't have a dog. Another good one is "This House Is Protected by a Silent Alarm." A thief who sees these signs will probably have second thoughts about breaking into a house, especially if there are other, unprotected houses nearby.

A corollary to this practice of putting up signs is a project known as *Operation Identification*. Under this program, police departments loan out engraving equipment to homeowners, who use the machines to engrave their social security numbers or names on their most valuable household objects, from TV sets to cameras and the bottoms of silverware. This means that anyone who tries to "fence" the objects after stealing them will have a harder time because they can so readily be traced, and because removal of the engraved names and numbers would leave the objects marked as suspicious. Homeowners who participate in Operation Identification receive stickers to put in their windows announcing that their possessions are marked. Reports indicate that people who participate have a significantly better chance of avoiding burglary than people who don't, and that when they are burglarized, their chances of getting back at least some of their possessions are improved. This might well be worth a try, and interested homeowners should contact their local police to inquire about Operation Identification.

However involved and expensive a security system may be, none has yet been found that is totally foolproof. Some of the ones that cost $100,000 and up are nearly foolproof, but they aren't very practical for the man or woman who lives in a $30,000 house and whose most expensive possession is a five-year-old color TV set. With security, as with everything else, the intelligent homeowner should first consider how much he can afford to pay, then consider his potential losses in a burglary, and finally make an investment in security which is sensible.

5

Security Packages You Can Afford

Thus far we have outlined what devices go into a security package. Security devices can be as simple as a padlock or a string of tin cans, or as complex as the latest electronic sensors. When a number of security devices are combined into a system to protect a single house or apartment, we refer to them as a *security package*.

In times such as our own, it goes without saying that every dwelling needs some kind of security package. The only problem involved with deciding on security is to figure out exactly how much security is desirable.

The two major factors in selecting a security package are: How much can you afford, and how much are you trying to protect? The security system that's completely adequate for a couple of students living in an efficiency apartment, a down-to-earth couple whose major possessions are probably hundreds of paperback books, would be totally inadequate for a socially prominent citizen whose home displays original Picassos and Dufys, silver service for twenty-four, antique firearms and furniture, and a whole panoply of goodies such as would tempt even an honest man to crime. For a home of the second type, the incredible array of electronic detectors now for sale might make a certain amount of sense. But it would be clearly illogical to spend a small fortune to protect an apartment full of moldy paperbacks and untyped term papers.

CALLING A CONSULTANT

Assuming that you do have a certain amount of valuable property in your home and want to install some expensive devices, it makes a good deal of sense to call in an expert security planner. The art of packaging various sensors and alarms into a system that does what it's supposed to has become a business for people experienced in electronics and security. Businesses that were once simple guard services— "rent-a-cop" agencies that provided uniformed men to protect high school dances and private beaches—have turned their attention to designing security systems for commercial and residential buildings. Even some locksmiths have taken up installing electronic systems as a sideline.

The reasons for such professional establishments, given the complexity of the electronic security field, are obvious, but a true story points them up clearly.

A series of burglaries had taken place in a quiet Midwestern neighborhood. One homeowner, who hadn't been broken into yet, decided he'd take no chances and went out to set up a security package for himself. He went to the local locksmith, who had a vast array of security devices for sale. The locksmith asked the homeowner if he knew what he was doing, and the man gruffly replied that he did and got some catalogs. A few days later he began to pick out devices like a kid at a candy store. He purchased about twenty sensors for the windows and doors, four ultrasonic motion detectors, some pressure switches, and a bell alarm. The bill for this, plus the wire necessary, came to several hundred dollars.

At home, the man read the instructions for each sensor and began to hook them up to his windows and doors. Toward the end of his wire-splicing odyssey however, he made a shocking discovery. Since the sensors were made by different man-

This display in a hardware store offers all the components of an electronic alarm system, but be sure you know what you're doing if you do it yourself. (Courtesy of Ed Hill.)

ufacturers, they wouldn't all work in the same system. In fact, about half the devices he had purchased were useless in concert with the other half.

The homeowner went to the locksmith to return the portion of equipment that was unusable. But the locksmith refused to accept the devices that had already been installed or removed from their packages. After initially losing his temper, the homeowner cooled off and began to talk with the locksmith about security systems. Eventually, he hired the locksmith to survey his home and recommend a security package and a technician to install the devices. Had he done this right off the bat, he could have saved several hundred dollars and a lot of aggravation.

The case for hiring a professional consultant is a strong one, but not without detracting points as well. On the positive side, the pro has a good working knowledge of the devices available and what they are capable of. He also knows their weak points. And he has seen enough homes to be able to save you money over what you would do yourself by telling you that certain expensive devices are not necessary for your own system or by steering you toward budget-priced items that are just as good for your purposes as the expensive ones.

The negative points depend on how good a consultant you come up with. By calling in any consultant, you have weakened your security system at least slightly, simply because there is now one person besides yourself who will know where your sensors are located. And if the consultant knows, and he works for a big company, everybody in his office will know, too. In any company, there is a chance that at least one person is dishonest and possibly even in collusion with burglars. So there is at least an outside chance of an inside job when you hire a consultant. For just this reason, you should seek out the consultant with a good reputation and an established company behind him.

Some consultants are not experts. In the home security field, where businesses are popping up like mushrooms after a summer rain, it's quite possible that you'll run into an "expert" who doesn't know much more than you do. But even if his advice is worthless, you'll still have to pay for it.

The fee is another consideration. A professional security expert might charge anywhere from $25 to $100 to make a survey of a house which might only take him ten to fifteen minutes. That's a lot of money for a small expenditure of time, especially if you don't have many valuable possessions to begin with. Of course, if you're planning to install a major security package, this price is only the beginning of a long and extensive financial relationship with the expert.

Last but not least, beware of the expert who is also a salesman and who tries to persuade you to buy specific brands of sensor or alarm. If he's getting a commission on a particular brand of device, you may wind up taking more sensors or alarms than you need or getting a brand that may not be as efficient as some other.

There are ways to cut corners on the price of security systems. If you have conducted an objective survey of your own, you may be able to eliminate the need for a professional survey and merely bring in the hired expert to hook up the alarm system. You may be able to obtain some help from the local police department. Some departments are glad to come out and survey your house for you, and to recommend the proper precautions.

When you decide that it's time to call the consultant, either before or after the survey, check the telephone book for a few names. Then call the Better Business Bureau and the police department to check the names, and ask each consultant to give you some reference. Ideally, they should have the names of a number of satisfied customers to use as references. When all the facts are in, you can pick out which consultant is best for you. But before signing anything, obtain in writing the price of a survey, if you're having it done, and also of the security package you want.

Remember, in deciding what sort of security package you want, that you yourself should be the judge. Don't bankrupt yourself paying for a security package designed to protect an embassy or an art museum if you have only a TV set and a radio that might be worth stealing. Budget your security package according to your life-style.

LOW-INCOME SECURITY

A family in southern New Jersey could barely afford the house they lived in, modest as it was. The husband was a factory worker and his wife stayed home with their five small children. They had never had much money, and with seven mouths to feed, the husband's paycheck barely covered the mortgage and food.

Unfortunately, though most of their neighbors were in the same economic boat, the neighborhood was plagued by burglaries. Half a dozen houses within a radius of a few blocks were plundered, and this didn't do the family's nerves any good.

Fear of burglary was a particular dilemma for a family that was barely making ends meet. If a thief did break in and make off with what few valuables they had—a TV, a radio, and a cheap record player—the family couldn't afford to replace them. They didn't want to take out extra insurance because they couldn't afford the premiums. And they felt that the price of security devices was far beyond them.

To make matters more frustrating, their yearly vacation was approaching and they had planned to spend one week in the country at a friend's cabin. But now they anticipated a week spent worrying about burglaries rather than enjoying themselves.

How could they protect their home adequately without spending too much money?

There are a number of security precautions within the reach of families in this income bracket which, while less costly than a sophisticated alarm system, are probably nearly as effective in protecting their few valuables and deterring a break-in.

The first step is to become friendly with your neighbors. If local relations are cordial, the neighbors may be willing to come to an agreement in which they will watch your home while you are out, and you can do the same for them. This results in a free sentinel service over the house to notice any strange noises, lights, or outward signs of burglary.

The next step is to stop by the local police stations and inform the police that you'll be leaving town on vacation. Ask the police to keep an eye on the house. If the department is properly run, the request will be passed on to the police officers who drive by the house three or four times a day. Some departments will have the men stop their patrol cars and walk around the house checking the windows and doors, which may detect a burglary in progress.

So far, without spending a dime, you have set up two different security systems for the house, with surveillance by the neighbors and police check-ups several times a day. This may well be more protection than the house was getting when you were home.

Next, cancel all the various home delivery services for the duration of your vacation. Stop off at the post office to ask them to hold your mail, call the newspaper to have your paper sent to your vacation address or held, and stop milk delivery. There's nothing more inviting to a burglar than to have a week's newspapers and mail lying around the front of the house, and sour milk in the milkbox can be a tip-off to burglars as well as a disgusting odor to the neighbors and to yourself when you come home.

Make sure that you leave some garbage in the garbage cans. Thieves have been known to check the garbage in garbage cans the night before the pick-up for your area, to see if there are any empty cans. An empty can is a tip-off that no one is home.

Now comes the creative part. Try to design a simple security device to protect each major entrance to your home. The trip string of empty cans across the inside of the door is one good example of a homemade device that can sometimes be very effective. Given the different layouts of homes, an inventive homeowner may come up with a better device than this for his particular need. Do *not*, however, try to set up any devices designed to kill or seriously injure a burglar. If these devices are effective and a burglar is actually harmed, he may be able to take you to court and win a suit against you, strange as it seems. The devices you work out for yourself should be noisemakers, not traps intended to kill or maim. If you rig up a device to rattle or smash when a burglar tries to get in, make sure you tell your neighbors what to listen for.

At this point, you have the neighbors and the police watching your house, no outward signs that you aren't at home, and noisemaking set up to make a quiet forcible entry impossible, all without spending a penny.

This may be enough to catch or ward off a thief. But at a cost of $6 to $10 more, you could make doubly sure by buying a light timer to switch your lights on and off and make sure that the thief who watches your home thinks somebody is home. The device should be set to turn a major light on at dusk and off at bed time.

Another ploy is to leave the radio playing. This may run up

a slight electric bill, but it will convince the average thief that somebody is home listening to the radio, and even if the thief rings the door and doesn't get an answer, he will probably be leery of breaking in. Moreover, the added electric bill caused by playing the radio will be cancelled out by the lights you would have used if you were at home instead of on vacation. Thus for about $7 a week, including the price of the light timer, the lower-income family could have purchased peace of mind for their week's vacation and protected their possessions.

MEDIUM INCOME

The main point to the lower-income security plan is, of course, its very cheapness, plus the fact that a burglar would probably be less obsessively interested in breaking into a lower-income family's home. One weakness, of course, is the reliance on neighbors, who, even if they are completely willing to help, may not be home a good deal of the time. Even if more than one neighbor is deputized for home surveillance, there will be times when the house isn't covered.

Informing the newsboy and the mailman that you won't be home is one way of disclosing that fact. It's better than letting the papers pile up on the doorstep and the letters jam the box, but it's still taking a chance on the reliability of the newsboy and the mailman, who may intentionally or unintentionally tip some felon off that you're not at home.

The basic weakness of the lower-income security package is the heavy reliance it places on the human element. People vary, and the lower-income package may be totally successful in some areas and totally ineffective in others, depending on the people involved.

The middle-income person, who can afford to invest a bit more than $10 in his home security, may be able to get into the electronic aspects of security and bypass some of the problems inherent in the cheaper security package, which relies almost totally on neighbors and the police.

Let's look at the middle-class person's life-style to see what kind of a package would be necessary. In all likelihood, most middle-income people don't have hugely expensive items around the house—diamond tiaras, original Rembrandts, Scythian goldware, and so forth. This doesn't mean they may not have a considerable investment tied up in their furniture, but thieves as a rule aren't interested in lugging away sofas and easy chairs. Because the middle-income person doesn't have many small, easily disposable objects of wealth around the house, he is probably interested mainly in detecting a thief when the thief breaks into the house, not when the thief stands in a specific place or enters a specific room. This means that your electronic surveillance will concentrate on the doors and windows.

The sensor of interest to the middle-income homeowner is the magnetic sensor that attaches to the doors and windows. A mild electric current will pass through this sensor at all times, and when the current flow is disrupted (by someone making entry) an alarm will go off. The middle-income person should consider the probable windows and doors through which a burglar would enter the house, and have a sensor attached to each of these. On most private houses, sensors on the doors and on the ground-floor windows will probably be sufficient. If a tree or some architectural foible of your house makes a second-floor window readily accessible, equip that one as well.

In an apartment on the first or second floor, it's probably best to protect all windows. On the third floor or above, it may be enough to put a sensor on the door and one on the window nearest the fire escape. These are the prime targets for a thief, if not the only ones.

The sensors should now be linked to an alarm. A bell alarm will probably serve adequately, and it is the cheapest. Make sure that the bell alarm is installed above the reach of a thief, even if he stands on a windowsill. The best place is over the highest window of the house. This will prevent the thief from disconnecting the wires or filling the bell with shaving cream to muffle the sound.

The police and neighbors should be informed that you now have an alarm system, and the neighbors should be asked to call the police if they hear the alarm bell clattering. It's also important that the police know you have an alarm so that if they hear it clanging a few houses or a few blocks away, they will know whose house is being broken into. If they don't know where the sound is coming from, it may take them some time to locate your house, and the burglar may have time to escape.

The total package of a bell alarm and a few sensors will cost anywhere from fifty to a few hundred dollars, depending on the number of sensors required and the type used. This might be exorbitant for a poor person, but it's probably well worth it to protect the kind of possessions that middle-income people acquire—cameras, tape recorders, several TVs, radios, and a hi-fi or stereo unit, kitchen appliances, family silver, and so forth. The average burglar, remember, is not a Monte Carlo jewel thief. He's perfectly satisfied to steal your kitchen appliances if you don't have any Cartier watches or rubies around. Considering the increased protection, then, it's probably worth the middle-class person's time to set up a simple electronic system. If you or a friend are really handy with electric appliances, you can hook up the sensors yourself. If you aren't handy, you can hire an electrician or locksmith to do the job for anywhere from $25 to $100. Always get a written estimate before signing an agreement or contracting the work. Once this package is installed, it requires little or no maintenance and should be pretty much self-sustaining.

As a corollary, you may want to ask a neighbor or a relative who lives nearby to pick up your mail and newspapers so that you don't have to let the post office and newspaper circulation department know that you are out. This will keep a tighter lid on your whereabouts and shut off at least one source of information to any potential burglar. Considering the convenience after installation and the relatively low cost, the system described is probably a good investment for a middle-income person.

UPPER-INCOME SECURITY

Those people who have been fortunate in finding the job that suits their nature perfectly, in having more than an average share of intelligence and drive, or maybe in just being born rich, usually acquire more valuable possessions than other, less fortunate people. "Collecting," after all, is one way in which a person who started out in straitened circumstances can storm the very pinnacles of Society with a capital S—provided that whatever he collects is valuable and interesting. And what is valuable and interesting to the general public is valuable and interesting to the thief.

If a thief can't simply push his way into a lower- or middle-income home, he's likely to forget the whole thing and move on to easier pickings. The same is not true to the house in the upper-income area, where the thief may know, or at least suspect, that the proceeds from a single night's work may enable him to relax for weeks, or even months. Therefore he is willing to take greater risks. A better class of neighbor, in a word, attracts a better class of burglar. Thus the methods of the middle-income security package may provide totally adequate security for the person of ordinary means, and from the garden-variety burglar, but they may not prove adequate to stop the truly determined and experienced thief who knows what he wants.

With the medium-priced package, sensors around the windows prevent the windows from being pried open. A skilled thief, however, can bypass this problem by taping over a ground-floor window with masking tape and breaking the glass. This causes the glass to smash with a muffled crunch and won't trigger the detector under most circumstances. The thief would only have to hit the glass once or twice, so that the neighbors couldn't tell which direction the sound came from even if they heard it. Unless they came out to investigate—and most neighbors wouldn't bother, whether from laziness or fear—the thief would then be at liberty to plunder the house.

Thus the wise upper-income person would supplement his sensors on each ground-floor window with ultrasonic motion detectors in each room. When testing the system out, you should be detected as soon as you enter any room. This should be linked to a silent alarm system which will tip off the police that someone has entered the house illegally. Thus they can approach the house and catch the burglar on his way out, taking a more-than-average-skilled criminal out of circulation for a while.

For added safety, pressure sensors should be installed near any valuable object—an original painting, a case of antique guns—under the rug on the way to the room where most of the valuables are kept. Thus even if the thief somehow eludes the motion detectors and the magnetic sensors on the windows, he will be picked up before he can make off with the real goodies.

A system this sophisticated shouldn't be linked to anything as simple as a bell alarm. The best idea is a silent alarm to the police station. If the police won't permit this for some reason, have the silent alarm linked to a guard service who can come to the scene themselves or summon the police, or have it linked with an automatic dialing system that will call the police and play a tape for them stating that a burglary is in progress.

For a system like this, you might expect to pay $550 to $1,000 for the equipment, with additional costs for installation, maintenance, and the electricity expended. You will have to pay a monthly charge to the telephone company for the silent alarm. The guard service, if used, would also charge a monthly service fee. The total cost might be around $1,200 for purchase and installation, and about $180 a year for maintenance. For the person of means, especially one who travels, the cost should be more than balanced out by the security and the peace of mind that a comprehensive system affords.

SECURITY FOR THE SUPER-RICH

The person who is really rich, as opposed to merely upper-income, has special problems with security. The rich family is almost certain to have expensive objects on their premises, perhaps in museumlike quantities. These are powerful incentives to a burglar. The rich usually have larger estates to protect, perhaps several acres of ground to be covered by security devices. When you live in a mansion 100 yards from the road, it's obviously impossible for a passing police car to see what's going on at your front door. The super-rich usually have servants, which increases the possibility of an inside job when it comes to burglary. Really, it's hard to blame some underpaid maid or scrubwoman for giving a thief a floor plan of the mansion for a cut of the take. The wonder is not that it happens, but that it happens so infrequently. And the super-rich are the logical targets of the elite of burglary, those romanticized crooks who actually plan their crimes in advance and use all sorts of special equipment.

Needless to say, the super-rich should take the same precautions as the upper-income people, with magnetic window sensors, pressure sensors under crucial spots, and motion detectors in the main rooms.

But that's just the beginning. Every item of extreme value should be fitted with a step-off pressure sensor to prevent a burglar from making off with a specific item when someone is home and the main system isn't activated. This technique may smack of the crude amateur, but remember, when the house alarm isn't activated, there's nothing to stop someone from simply smashing his way in and making off with that priceless oil painting or gold art object.

Every employee the family hires to work around the house should be completely investigated by a private investigation service, and not hired until all the facts are in.

The family should hire a security guard for the driveway and grounds. This guard should check up on anyone found in the area and all visitors, and announce their presence at the front door before they enter the house.

Ultrasonic movement detectors should be installed around the grounds and programmed so as not to activate at the sound of branches moving in the wind. These will inform the people at home of any movement in the yard at night and warn them of the stealthy approach of any burglar or other malefactor. Sensors should also be placed on a fence around the house and linked either to the main house or the guard's house. This is to prevent a signal from going out to the police every time a naughty boy or a cat climbs over the wall. A few incidents like this, as in Aesop's fable of "The Boy Who Cried Wolf," and the police might be desensitized to the alarm system through answering too many false alarms. A local sensor system should report directly to the guard on the premises with a light at a control panel showing the exact location of the break-in.

Electricity for this ideal security system would be provided by a separate generator which would turn on if anything happened to the main (public) electric source. In this way, a thief cannot immobilize electrically operated sensors simply by cutting a power line. The same electrical sources that power the sensors would power the lights that illuminate the outside of the house and the grounds.

The best place for jewelry, other than on a beautiful woman, is in a bank's insured safety deposit vault. But if you must keep the jewelry at home, make sure that it is kept in a safe, one heavy enough not to be movable without heavy equipment such as a tank rescue vehicle or a railroad crane. Believe it or not, there have been reports of thieves breaking into a mansion and removing the safe with pulleys. So the heavier the safe, the better.

To prevent an inside job in which an employee turns off the security system, it would be advisable to have two systems, with different sensors. With a dual system, one security package would rely mainly on magnetic window and door detectors, while the second system would rely on pressure sensors protecting each important object. Each system would be individually powered. Thus, if a thief were helped by an employee who shut off the magnetic detector system, he could still fall afoul of the pressure detector system.

On the face of it, a system like this may seem like something out of James Bond, but for the homeowner with a million dollars locked up in his house, grounds, and property, it would seem a small investment. A system like this might cost $15,000 to $30,000 for initial installation and $15,000 a year to maintain (most of it for the guard service), and even this is not the outer limit. A newly successful moviemaker recently paid $100,000 for a security system for his home. Understandably, he refuses to discuss the exact details and components of this security package, but he claims that former agents from both the CIA and the FBI failed to penetrate his system.

6

You, the Thief, and the Law

KNOW YOUR RIGHTS

Burglary and its attendant practices are obviously illegal, as everyone, including the thief, is fully aware. But most non-criminals don't realize the maze of legal technicalities that have grown up around theft and burglary. Many of these laws are quite natural outgrowths of the United States Constitution's attempts to ensure every citizen equal justice under the law, but they have proliferated to such an extent that they may actually trip up the law-abiding citizen and place him at the mercy of the criminal in a court of law.

Without undue meditation on the irony of the situation, we must consider the specific guarantees of the Constitution as they apply to you, the homeowner, and also to the burglar you may someday have to deal with.

Under the Constitution, you have the right to privacy in your home and to freedom from unlawful search and seizure of your belongings. This protection applies not only to the actions of law officers and police, but also to those of private citizens. A reporter, for instance, doesn't have the right to enter your home and look around without your permission.

Needless to say, the same stricture that applies to law-abiding citizens applies to burglars. The only time that any person may legally enter your home and remove your possessions is when a court order has been issued. This may occur if you haven't paid your rent or mortgage, or if your landlord has some other valid reason for eviction. Court orders are also required for searching a home or for tapping a telephone.

The various states also have laws against illegal entry into homes or removal of property. So the homeowner's right to his personal privacy and his possessions is protected both by the United States Constitution and the law of the state he resides in. The homeowner has the right to protect his home by using whatever force is required to safeguard his life and his family's lives and his possessions. However, the phrase "whatever force is required" is a crucial one: exerting more force than is "required" may make the homeowner criminally liable.

Strange as it may seem, especially to fans of Western and police movies and TV shows, there is no guaranteed right of a homeowner to gun down anyone who happens to barge into his house. In many states a person who fires a gun at a thief who has entered his home is overstepping his legal rights and may be held liable for his actions. The thief may actually sue for attempted murder if a homeowner shoots and wounds him. If the thief is killed, his family could charge the homeowner with second degree murder or manslaughter, and sue for damages. Cases such as this have actually gone to court and sometimes have been decided in the deceased felon's favor.

On the other hand, if the thief is armed with a gun, killing him is clearly a case of self-defense. If a thief attacked you with a knife, or even with his fists, and you shot him, you would probably be acquitted in court if charged. Reasonable force is determined by the situation, and it is quite reasonable for a man who is in danger of death or injury to defend himself by killing his assailant. In other cases, there is a fine line which would have to be determined by a jury. For instance, if a thief is fleeing the scene of a break-in with a prized possession, and you hit him with a chair and kill him, are you guilty of murder, of manslaughter, or merely acting within your constitutional rights to defend your property?

Using a chair may not be an orthodox method, but the private citizen does, in fact, have a clear right to make an arrest. A citizen's arrest, often spoken of with a certain disbelief, is perfectly legal. If a thief is cornered in your house and you think you can stop him and hold him until the police arrive, you simply inform him that he is under arrest. Stopping him from escaping, of course, may be slightly more difficult. After the police arrive, you must sign a complaint charging the thief with breaking and entering.

In questions of how much force is justified, the usual answer is that the proper amount of force is dictated by the situation. A rule of thumb could be that the homeowner has the right to use the same amount of force as the thief. If the burglar has a knife, you are justified in using a knife. If the burglar has a gun, you are justified in using a gun. In practice, of course, nobody but Joel McCrea playing Buffalo Bill will enter a fight by throwing away his gun and whipping out a knife so as to be on equal terms with his adversary—Anthony Quinn playing Chief Yellow Hand, in this case. Things like that used to happen in Hollywood movies, though probably not in the Old West the movies claim to portray. They certainly don't happen in suburbia. The whole point of the reasonable-force debate is that you can get in very serious legal trouble by shooting an unarmed burglar, especially if he's outside your house running away.

Thus, the homeowner's rights are simple: He has the right to defend himself with reasonable force, to make an arrest of a felon, and to sign a complaint charging another person with a crime. There may be other rights or restrictions beyond these, depending on the state that the homeowner lives in.

THE THIEF'S RIGHTS

Oddly enough, the thief is guaranteed the same basic constitutional rights as the homeowner. He too may protect himself from violence with reasonable force, may charge anyone with a crime, and may arrest anyone who is committing a crime.

These rights play an important part in any confrontation between a thief and a homeowner. The mere fact that a person is a professional thief does not place him outside the law where his human rights are concerned. The days when people were officially declared outlaws and others could kill them with impunity—a custom that stems from the Vikings—are mercifully over, and none too soon. They may have seemed romantic in retrospect, but the problem was that the wrong people got killed much too often.

The concept of equal protection under law means equal protection for everybody. If you see a known thief walking through your backyard, for instance, and fire a gun at him, you yourself are guilty of a serious crime, since the thief's crime in walking through your yard, trespassing, is a very minor one and in no way justifies using the thief for target practice. Unless you actually see the thief breaking into a house or apartment, all you can legally do is question him, and, if you are suspicious, call the police. Anything beyond that would be interfering with the thief's civil rights, and you could be held liable for this in court.

Another tantalizing situation is one in which the thief is observed walking around a neighborhood ringing doorbells to find a house to break into. Although a private citizen or policeman who sees the thief doing this may know what is happening, the thief has the right to do this, and he cannot be arrested until he breaks into a home. In a town which requires a solicitor's permit, of course, he probably wouldn't be doing this, and if he were, his permit could be revoked.

Some years ago there was an incident in the Midwest in which an elderly couple set a shotgun trap for a thief who had plagued them and their friends. This device is a variation of the spring gun that English landowners used to set for poachers: one end of a string or wire is attached to the trigger of a shotgun and the other to some object. When the string is stretched taut, the shotgun discharges, and pellets hit the person who has dislodged the string.

The elderly couple tied one end of their string to a window sash. One night while they were asleep, a thief came to the window, which they had left slightly ajar. As he lifted the window to enter the house, the shotgun blasted him.

This might seem like poetic justice, especially to someone who had been a victim of burglaries. But the thief sued the elderly couple in court and beat them. They were actually forced to sell their house to pay for damages. The thief, however, was himself convicted of breaking and entering.

Part of the court's justification for convicting the old couple was that the shotgun trap endangered others besides the thief. A child could have come to the window or a policeman could have been checking out the house, and the shotgun would have impartially blasted them as easily as the burglar.

Interestingly enough, a similar case in England two decades ago had an opposite verdict. In this case, a mechanic whose tools had periodically been stolen, set up a spring gun covering the tool chest of his garage. A burglar tried to pry open the tool chest and was all but cut in half by the shotgun blast. The mechanic was charged with murder but was acquitted because the garage was an extension of his house, and, as we all

A dangerous (and illegal) shotgun trap. The string to the window pulls the trigger if the window is opened. Using a device like this can lead to massive legal troubles or potential tragedy. (Courtesy of Mike SanGiovanni.)

know, an Englishman's home is his castle. It says something about the attitudes of England and America that the English have unarmed police but justify a homeowner's shooting even a nonviolent criminal on his property.

It is axiomatic that a man is innocent until proven guilty. We wouldn't really want it any other way. But this, too, can have some serious consequences for the homeowner who tries to protect his property.

Consider the case of the man who signs a complaint against a thief. The accused thief goes before several judicial bodies and has his day, or days, in court. If the case is thrown out of court or the accused thief is found not guilty, the person you accused can sue you and possibly collect damages for false arrest. This charge may be augmented with a charge of defamation of character. Thus if you bring charges against a thief, but the prosecution cannot prove beyond a reasonable doubt that he is guilty, you may wind up on the receiving end of the legal system—you, that is, receiving the charges while the thief hopes to be receiving your money.

Thus you should make very sure that you have all the facts straight before charging anyone with theft or any other crime or before attempting a citizen's arrest. Innocent homeowners have become the defendants in many cases because they unknowingly violated the rights of a thief or because they failed to produce sufficient evidence against a thief.

CONFRONTING THE THIEF

We have already mentioned that the thief usually tries to avoid confronting the homeowner at all costs. But there are times when, through an oversight or an accident, a homeowner and a thief may bump into one another head-on, which will probably cause both of them a great deal of consternation. This is a crucial moment for the homeowner, and he should act rationally and coolly. Taking the proper steps can save a life—yours or the thief's—and lead to the conviction of a criminal as well. A blunder could cause a death—perhaps your own.

First and foremost, however, you should try to avoid a

confrontation with a burglar. The burglar may be young and inexperienced or a bitter drug addict afraid of going back to jail, and in a moment of rage or panic, he may be quite capable of murder or mayhem. Then again, you yourself may fly into a rage when you find your home desecrated and pillaged and be capable of some mayhem yourself, which could potentially be held against you in court. So avoiding a showdown is the wisest course.

There are telltale signs to look for on returning home from any extended absence—"extended" being the minimum time it would take a thief to break into your house. If the thief has entered through the front door, the door might show signs of forcible entry, such as chisel marks or breakage around the lock, or it may be left open. If you find this, be on the alert. A thief may still be inside. If you notice any of these signs, don't enter the house or apartment. If the thief hears you coming and is trapped inside, he may wait in ambush to club or stab you before escaping. The best course is to go to a neighbor's house or a pay phone and call the police. Then wait outside until the police arrive.

If, however, you find no signs but enter the house and find a burglar inside, back off as quickly as possible. Don't attack the burglar unless he attacks you first. There have been cases of a

A patrolman frisks a suspect against a car after apprehending him. (Courtesy of Mike SanGiovanni.)

resident pulling a gun on an unarmed burglar and then having the gun taken away from him and used on him. There have also been cases of homeowners facing serious criminal charges for killing an unarmed felon inside their homes. Don't try to play police. It's not your job.

Instead of attacking, give the thief enough room to get past you and out of the house. Don't back him into a corner or try to seize him. Unobtrusively study his face and physique so that you can provide information to the police later. The height is very important and so are any scars or other visible characteristics that set the thief apart from the general populace.

Follow the thief's instructions if he tells you to stand back and let him pass or warns against following him. It's not your job to get killed playing Matt Dillon or Wyatt Earp. All the thief probably wants at this point is to make a clean getaway, and it's in your best interest to let him do so. Retribution will come later. As soon as you are sure the thief is gone, call the police and give them a full description. They will transmit this information to all patrol cars, and they should immediately converge on your neighborhood and start looking for the perpetrator. If the thief used a car, of course, and you got a look at it, tell the police this information, too. Best of all is to have the license number, though the car may have been stolen from an innocent homeowner like yourself for the caper.

Once you have summoned the police, stay at home until they arrive. While waiting for them, write down the fullest description you can of the thief, the exact time you saw him, and a list of whatever you think he took.

If you follow these instructions, you'll be safe and you'll also help capture the thief and make sure that he is convicted. There have been many times when a resident was so shaken that she couldn't give an adequate description of the thief she bumped into, and the thief was released to go on plundering.

EVIDENCE

You should have begun collecting evidence as soon as you bumped into the thief—very basic evidence, such as his height, weight, complexion, approximate age, hair and eye color, and any visible scars. His clothing is also important if he is caught immediately, before he has had a chance to go home and change.

From here, the quality of the police department will come into focus. If the police force is a truly professional one, they will ask you to come down to headquarters and use your description of the thief's physical features to make up a composite sketch of the man. Some bigger forces keep an artist on tap to do this sort of work. Others have a book with dozens of sets of eyebrows, dozens of noses, and so forth, which can be manipulated to provide a reasonable likeness of the thief. Once this picture is completed, the police will distribute it to all their officers and perhaps to other departments.

After you have given the description, several police officers will arrive at your apartment or house and begin to ask you questions and search for evidence. The first thing they will probably want, other than a description, is the method used by the thief to gain entry into the apartment. This may be important in establishing the thief's M.O. (*modus operandi*, or method of operating) which can be a clue to his identity. If a tool was used to force entry, the police may take a plaster cast of it so that if they catch a likely suspect, they can match the marks of his tools with the marks they have casts of.

The next step will be to look for fingerprints. Unlike the detectives on TV and the movies, police can usually obtain prints from a limited number of places. The best prints will come from shiny smooth surfaces—linoleum counters, glass, steel—or from greasy surfaces. You can help the police by trying to remember whether or not the thief touched any place likely to take a good fingerprint. If he did, and you can remember, it will help the police save time and effort. Of course, if the thief happened to be a fastidious type and was wearing gloves, you can tell this to the police and save them a lot of time and effort right there.

After looking for fingerprints, the police probably will look around outside in the garden for footprints. If you tell them how the thief left the house and which way he seemed to be heading, this will be a great help to them. Again, if they find any likely tracks, they may make plaster casts. They will also

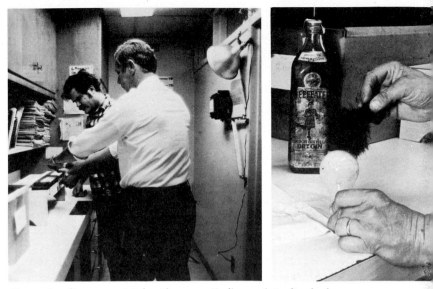

Above: A police sergeant takes the suspect's fingerprints, for checks with other departments and the FBI. (Courtesy of Mike SanGiovanni.) Above, right: A police detective dusts a light bulb for fingerprints after a burglary. (Courtesy of Mike SanGiovanni.)

probably want to match your shoes and those of your family with the footprints they cast, just to make sure that they aren't looking at your own tracks.

The police will also want to know what, if anything, was stolen from your house. This may well prove to be the most important part of the investigation, because unless the police can prove that you had the items to begin with, they may not be able to get them back for you even if they locate them.

To make the policemen's job easier, you should keep an inventory list which includes the serial numbers of all the important possessions in your home—TV, radio, stereo, cameras, binoculars, guns, and so forth. Articles that don't have serial numbers should have your social security number carved into them. Of course, if you belong to Operation Identification or some such plan in which all your possessions are marked, this will make matters simpler. If, for instance, the thief is caught nearby, if he fits the description you have given, and if the police find items you have described (with proper serial numbers) in his possession, he will have a very hard time talking his way out of town. Thus, a clear identification of all your possessions is very important to catching a thief, and to making sure that he's taken out of circulation for a while.

THE ARREST

When the police have the description and all other relevant information, they will implement a search for the thief. Depending on how smart the thief is and how efficient the police are, they may be able to apprehend him before he gets out of the neighborhood. When the police stop the thief in his car, they will look in the backseat for any stolen merchandise, and if they find it, they will probably take the thief into the station house for questioning. If they think they have enough evi-

Police bring a handcuffed suspect to the police station. (Courtesy of Mike SanGiovanni.)

dence, they will arrest him there. In the meantime, they may get a search warrant signed by a judge to open the trunk of the car.

At this point, you may be asked to go down to the police station to identify the suspect. This may be done at a classic "lineup" in which the suspect and some other men are marched past with bright lights shining on them, or it may be in a much more informal setting. If you are afraid for your safety, insist that you be allowed to observe the suspect from a vantage point where you yourself can't be seen by him. If you can readily identify the suspect as the thief, do so. If you can't or aren't sure, tell the police this, too. From here on, what happens is largely up to them.

Once the suspect has been identified, he will be taken to another room and forced to remove his clothing for a thorough search. He will be photographed and a photo will be sent to the FBI, the state police, the county police, and the local police file. These photos will remain in the files even if the person is found not guilty or the case is thrown out of court. After the photograph, the suspect will be fingerprinted and the prints will also be sent to various files.

The suspect is then housed in the local jail until the police are ready for more intensive questioning. This may take a half hour, and the person is read his rights and given the right to call a lawyer if he wishes. If he cannot afford one, the court will appoint one from the Public Defender's office. The suspect is then questioned and has the right to refuse to answer. After the questioning, the suspect is brought back to jail to wait until a judge sets bail. This may take anywhere from an hour or two to a few days.

When bail is set, the suspect may leave jail if he can meet the bail. He may call a *bondsman*, who makes it his profession to bail people out of jail and then collects the interest on the bail money. If the suspect cannot raise money, he must remain in jail until his trial. If he puts up bail, the money will be refunded to him after the trial, whether he is acquitted or convicted. If he flees without waiting for trial, however, the bail is forfeited.

The accused thief begins his days in court with a pretrial

A suspect is photographed for ID at the police station. (Courtesy of Mike SanGiovanni.)

A suspect is frisked in the cellblock before being jailed prior to arraignment. (Courtesy of Mike SanGiovanni.)

hearing before the municipal judge of the community in which he was arrested. If the charges against him are serious, he may be remanded to a grand jury trial at the county level; if the grand jury thinks the evidence sufficient, he will get a trial in which twelve jurors selected from the public are called upon to rule on his guilt or innocence. This process can take up to a year or possibly even more, and during this time the defendant is usually free on bail. In fact, he may even be out burglarizing houses again while he waits for his trial to come up.

You, as a homeowner, will probably be required to appear at the preliminary hearing, which will most likely mean spending an evening in court, waiting for your turn to come up. You will be placed under oath and asked questions by the prosecutor and the defense attorney.

If the case goes to the county prosecutor after the grand jury meets on it, you will also probably have to go to the prosecu-

A suspect in a local police station cell: paying the penalty of an unsuccessful break and entry. (Courtesy of Mike SanGiovanni.)

tor's office and answer some more questions. This will probably take place during normal working hours, so be prepared to miss a day of work if you are asked to appear.

Then comes the trial—"Perry Mason" time—though undoubtedly less dramatic than the TV dramas most people associate with courtroom protocol. Here you will have to answer the same questions all over again. This will probably consume a few more days of your working time. Your principal job in testifying will be to tell the simple truth and to identify any items that were stolen from your house or apartment. After all the trials are over, you will get these objects back, if you haven't already.

If the accused thief is convicted and his lawyer appeals the conviction, you may have to go to yet another appeal trial and testify again.

When called on to testify each time, you will receive a subpoena, handed to you by a court officer or policeman. This is nothing more than an official reminder that you have an appointment to testify, so don't panic when you receive one—it's not an indication that you've done anything wrong.

When you actually do go up to testify, you will probably be sworn in with one hand on a *Bible*. This is a formality, but don't take it lightly, even if you aren't especially religious. If you are caught lying under oath, you can be charged with perjury, which is a fairly serious offense. You may wind up in custody yourself. Just tell the truth as simply as possible. The defense attorney may try to confuse you or get you to admit things that aren't true. Don't take this personally; it's part of his job. But don't yield one inch from reporting exactly what happened.

As you can see, the court system, which is devised to protect the rights of all citizens, can be a pain in the neck to the law-abiding homeowner who just wants to mind his own business and be secure in his own life and property. That is why it's a good idea to take every reasonable precaution to ensure that you aren't burglarized in the first place.

7

How to Spot
a Suspicious Person
and What to Do

As we have previously discussed, the average burglar doesn't just charge up to a house and burst in like Santa Anna storming the Alamo. If he did, he would probably be caught within a matter of hours, and other burglars would shun him as a madman. The burglar, whether he is a skilled cracksman or a relatively bumbling amateur, usually devotes a lot more time to *casing*, or sizing up, a house than he does to the actual break and entry and larceny. And it's during this time that an alert homeowner or apartment dweller can take steps to fend the thief off or even to get him arrested and put away.

Spotting the burglar is thus crucial to stopping him. If the burglars that work the streets in real life looked like the crooks in old Dick Tracy comic strips—porky figures in pullovers with jutting, stubbled chins and little black raccoon masks—spotting them would be easy. Unfortunately, they don't, nor do they come in any particular age, shape, or color. Any person between puberty and senility may be a burglar, and he doesn't wear a mask.

Police officers are trained to detect and observe suspicious persons though, of course, they cannot make an arrest without reasonable cause, no matter how clearly the suspicious person's actions may stamp him as a thief on the make. They have to keep watching until the thief makes a move and breaks the law before they can move in and make a pinch. Forearmed with some of the same tips that the police have, you can spot the burglars yourself and take precautions of your own.

IN APARTMENTS

Whatever the relative merits of a house against an apartment in terms of economy and convenience, apartment dwellers are at a considerable disadvantage in the spotting of burglars right at their front door. Quite simply, the homeowner knows that, beyond friends and the mailman, nobody has a reason to be loitering anywhere in the vicinity of his front door. The apartment dweller can make no such assumption, especially if he lives in a big apartment house with dozens or hundreds of tenants.

Most people who live in an apartment building don't know all or even most of the people who live in the building. The very physical closeness of people who live in the same apartments seems to encourage a sort of aloof detachment from neighbors. People who have lived a few feet away for years may barely speak to one another and may consciously or subconsciously take pains to avoid any intimacy.

Just because of this factor, as well as because of the transient nature of apartment dwelling, strange faces in the building don't usually arouse much curiosity. Apartment residents simply pay no attention when they see a stranger walking around the hall. Thus a thief who walks around as if he owned the place, or as if he had business there, can avoid any suspicion from all but the most paranoid apartment dwellers. The skilled thief may even reassure a resident he meets with a smile.

There is no easy answer to the problem of spotting thieves in an apartment house. But there are some precautions that may help.

First, when you move into an apartment, try to get to know

some of the residents, your new neighbors. If you can't get to meet each person who lives in the building, at least try to remember faces you see regularly in the hall. This will enable you to pick out any strange faces you meet in the hall. Hopefully, at least some of your neighbors will be checking out your face at the same time, for the same reason.

If you can remember faces, half the battle is won. While entering and leaving the building, take notice of the faces around you, both inside and outside the building. If you see any that don't belong there, contemplate some sort of action.

However, the action you contemplate shouldn't be confrontation. This is the last thing you would want to do. You're not a policeman, and trying to play cop can be dangerous. If you spot an unfamiliar face that really doesn't seem to belong in the building, proceed quietly to your destination, either to your apartment or to whatever outside place you're going to. When you arrive, call the superintendent of the building and inform him or her of the situation. This will protect you physically and legally from the consequences of getting directly embroiled with a possible burglar—or with an innocent bystander.

Though few residents would be likely to sue you for asking them if they lived in the building, they wouldn't be legally obligated to answer either. You have no legal right to question people if you are merely a tenant. The only person who can legally question someone on the apartment's premises is the owner of the building or his or her agent. This means the superintendent has the legal right to question anyone strolling through the halls, but you don't.

If, for any reason, you can't reach the superintendent, and you are fairly sure that the person you've observed doesn't belong in the building, call the police. Just tell them what the situation is, and they should take it from there. Usually, the police will arrive a few minutes after your call and enter the building. If they find someone hanging around the halls, they will question him; if the suspect turns out to be an innocent bystander, nothing will happen to him. If he really is a thief, he probably won't be apprehended, but you can be reasonably sure that he'll give your building a wide berth in the future.

ON THE STREET

The person who lives in a one- or two-family house has no corridors or halls to serve as a detection zone for burglars. So the methods he has to use to detect a thief are somewhat different from those used by the apartment dweller.

A thief who is trying to break into a private house doesn't usually observe the home from the property itself. This is not only a very obvious and suspicious way to case a house, but legally foolish as well; by trespassing on private property, the thief would be laying himself open to prosecution. The thief who wants to break into a private house does his casing from the street.

For the thief, the street is the perfect position. If he's on foot, he can stroll gallantly by several times, making mental notes each time he passes the house. No one will usually notice this kind of stroll, at least not in a good-sized town. Most people don't sit around watching the street, and even if they see the thief, they'll assume that he's just out for a walk.

The thief is equally likely to use a car to case the houses in a given area. If he sees a house that looks good, he may stop the car and sit there a while. Most people who see him will probably assume he's waiting for someone to come out of one of the houses. If he thinks that sitting in the car may arouse suspicion, he may even get out and pretend to tinker with the engine. Everybody has car trouble now and then.

For the homeowner, of course, this "car trouble" could be the prelude to burglary.

The homeowner, like the apartment dweller, should cultivate a memory for faces in his immediate neighborhood. Of course, if he's friendly with all or most of his neighbors, matters are a lot simpler. When everyone knows everyone else, it's easy to spot a stranger. The homeowner should also try to remember cars on the block. This isn't so that he can envy the man with a Rolls-Royce or look down on the man with a blown-out '48 De Soto. It's so he can know which cars are out-of-place when left on the street.

Once you've memorized the faces and the cars on your block, keep your eyes open for strange faces and strange cars. When you see a face or a car that you don't recognize, observe it closely. If the person or car is around for an inordinate amount of time, do something about it. If, for instance, you see a strange car parked in front of your neighbors' house and you know that they're on vacation, or out for the evening, it's worth a call to the police just to be on the safe side.

When walking to or leaving your home, unobtrusively check on the parked cars you pass. Is there someone sitting inside? If so, especially if it seems to be only one person, this is suspicious, and action should be taken.

In some situations, of course, the person in the parked car will turn out to be a relative or friend of the family. But you can't assume that this will always be the case. Police questioning won't hurt an innocent person. In fact, if the police *don't* question people sitting around in parked cars, there's something wrong with the police protection in the neighborhood. Don't be afraid to take the lead in demanding proper police protection for yourself and your neighbors by insisting on a rigorous police patrol of residential areas. In the long run, the police will benefit as well, since patrolling will give them a chance to show their worth and is certainly less boring than sitting around the police station.

AT YOUR DOOR

One of the favorite techniques of the day burglar, as we have discussed, is to go from door to door posing as a salesperson in his quest for unoccupied houses to break into. So the aggravation that many people feel at being disturbed by a door-to-door salesperson may be even greater if the "salesperson" calls while they're away and plunders their house. People more sinister than ordinary burglars—armed robbers or sexual deviates—have sometimes used the same ploy to gain entry to homes. So you never really know what to expect when the doorbell rings.

One solution to this problem, if you have a big dog, is to send him to answer the door. Most door-to-door people have a dread of large dogs and when they see yours jumping around like a lion ready to pounce, they may not need a second invitation to bug out. This may seem terribly rude to ladies and gentlemen of the old school, but after all, you didn't ask the salesperson to come around ringing your doorbell, did you?

If you decide to see the person at the door, first of all remember: Don't give any indication that you're home alone, if you are a woman. Say something like "Please talk quietly. My husband's working the night shift this week and he's sleeping." Or "My husband and I were just getting ready to go out, so you'll have to excuse me for not asking you in." Keep the person at the door, outside the house, and don't let him get inside the door. Real salespeople, if they are experienced, are used to this and understand your reasons for doing so. If the "salesperson" is in fact a thief, he'll also understand and realize he's not dealing with an easy victim.

The first thing to do with a "salesperson" is to look and see if he's carrying samples of the product he's selling. If he doesn't have either samples or a catalogue clearly visible, you can assume right there that something is funny. After all, how can a salesperson sell a product if he doesn't have anything to show you?

Even if he does have samples this, of course, is only a slight improvement. A smooth thief may carry phony samples around with him. He may even have goods with him that he has stolen from a nearby house and may be passing these off as samples. Thieves have also been known to steal merchandise in transit and pass this off as samples, or to try to peddle it to homeowners. Thus samples, while they may be convincing to some, are no proof.

A better evidence of good faith is a canvassing permit. If your town requires door-to-door salespeople to register with the police and obtain a permit, ask to see it. If they can present a permit, their claims may be seen in a somewhat more sympathetic light. Most thieves, after all, aren't about to let themselves be fingerprinted and checked through state or federal files to obtain a permit when they can find other towns to canvass that don't require this. If you want to be doubly sure, read the name on the permit and then ask the salesperson to wait outside the house. Lock the door behind you, go inside, and call the police to ask if they've issued a permit to the person whose name is on the permit. If they say they have, you can be at least 98 percent sure that the salesperson is legitimate. If the police haven't issued the permit, you can be 98 percent sure that the "salesperson" won't be there when you go to the door.

If the police should inform you that they never issued the permit, try to get back to the door in time to see which direction the bogus salesperson is fleeing in. If you can get a description of the car he may be using, especially of the license plate, this may be invaluable. Inform the police of the situation, and describe the person.

Your community, unfortunately, may not have a law requiring permits for soliciting or selling door-to-door. If they don't, ask to see the salesperson's business card. This will have a name, the name of a business, and the phone number on it. Again, ask the salesperson to wait outside while you step in to check up on the information. This time, don't simply call the number on the business card; the clever thief may have an accomplice waiting at the number on the card to answer the phone and give you a line of baloney about the imaginary company. Instead of falling for this ruse, call up Information and ask for the company's phone number. If it is listed, you can probably trust the salesperson not to be a burglar. If it is *not* listed, call the police and let the salesperson do the explaining to them.

Another ploy the thief may use to check out your house is to pose as a wayfarer who is either lost or having car trouble. If such a person comes to your door, don't let him in. If he asks for your address, give it to him but ask whom he wanted to speak to or see. If he gives a name you've never heard of, especially if it's a super-common name like Smith or Jones, try to check his license number and call the police as soon as he's gone. *Don't* let him into the house under any circumstances. Pretending to be lost may be a very amateurish ploy, but the amateurs in crime are usually the most dangerous. If he insists that he has to make a phone call, take down the number for him and make the call yourself, while he waits safely outside a locked door. Or offer to call the police and ask their help. This should really separate the thieves from the honest people.

ON THE TELEPHONE

At some point everybody has gotten an unwanted telephone call. It may be some squeaky-voiced kid who calls up to ask for a friend, it may be a salesman who's gotten your phone number from some sucker list and calls to try to unload some Florida estates, or it may be a pervert who gets his kicks calling people up and cursing at them or just breathing into the receiver.

And then again, it may be a burglar.

Detection over the telephone is somewhat more complicated than detection in person. You can't see the person who is calling you, which may be just as well. Who the heck wants people staring at them when they've just climbed out of bed or the bathtub? TV-phones are said to be on the way, but to those of us who cherish our privacy, this seems more like a technological invasion than a boon to humanity. It may also make it easier for thieves, by giving them a chance to case the place they plan to hit by phone.

In any case, there are a few things to remember about burglary when talking on the telephone. When you answer the telephone, try to remember the name of the person who calls and the name of the company he claims to represent. Let the person give you a sales pitch while you concentrate on remembering his name. At the end of the call, repeat the name of his business but give his name wrong. If the caller is for real, he'll correct you immediately. But if your caller is a thief, he may have forgotten the name himself and agree with you. Or you can mix up the name of the service company and see if he catches you then.

Never give out information about yourself or any member of your family over the telephone. You never know whom you're talking to, and the caller might not only be a thief but a pervert as well.

Be especially leery of letting out any information about when you will or won't be home. Don't ever tell anyone who calls you when you'll be away so he can break into your house. The thief may pose as someone trying to set up appointments for personal visits and ask if you're available to meet with him on Wednesday night. If you say "No, we'll be going out that night," or "We'll be on vacation," he has all the information he needs to execute a break-in with almost total confidence. A better ruse on your part is either to say nothing at all or to say, "No, we'll be having company that night."

Needless to say, this goes for your friends' schedules as well. If a thief disguised as a salesperson calls and asks whether you think your next door neighbors would be interested in meeting him and you tell him they're on vacation, you've just about hung a "Rob Me" sign on their door. Remember, if you tell a caller when your neighbors will be home, you've also told him, by the process of elimination, when they won't be home.

Sometimes a thief will merely call the house to see if anyone is home and will hang up as soon as someone picks up the receiver. This can also be an innocent mishap—some honest person may dial a wrong number and be too embarrassed to apologize—but if you get a number of phone calls when no one answers as you pick up the receiver, it's a suspicious circumstance and may well mean that somebody is planning to burglarize your house. If you get a series of calls where the caller hangs up, call both the police and the telephone company.

WORKERS BY YOUR NEIGHBOR'S HOUSE

Most of us are used to seeing crews of workmen around the neighborhood, fixing roofs, installing siding, landscaping, or perhaps working on leaders and gutters. Few people would even think to question their appearance.

But on some occasions, these supposedly hardworking people are really thieves who have donned the clothing of honest workmen like the wolf in sheep's clothing.

A few years ago, in New York City, some workmen were disgorged from a moving truck and walked boldly into a school building. They went up to a second-floor classroom, took out a few windows, and removed a 9-foot grand piano by hauling the instrument out the window. The school security guard, being an amiable man, helped the movers pack the piano up. Faculty members on the street watched the piano movers calmly, no doubt quietly thankful that they didn't have to haul pianos for their daily bread. The men finished their arduous chore and drove away.

It wasn't until months later that anyone noticed that the piano had never been returned. The men in mover's clothes had acutally been thieves.

No one had questioned the men because the men were not conspicuous by their stealth. They looked as though they belonged there. Everyone knew that from time to time pianos were moved from the building for repair, and they assumed that this was just more of the same.

The same ploy is used to plunder businesses and residential buildings. Movers and repairmen are always working around houses and shops, and some of them may well be thieves, too.

Ideally, you and your neighbors should let one another know if you or they intend to have movers or a repair crew around. If there is a repair crew roaming a neighborhood and no one knows who asked them to come, a call to the police may not be out of line. If you see repairmen stop off at a neighbor's house and you know that no one is home, watch to see if they enter the house. Be especially curious to see if they use a key to open the door or if they employ some slightly more esoteric method. If they kick the door in or rip it off the hinges, a call to the police is mandatory. Meanwhile, try to check out the license plate and the color and make of the truck they arrived in for future use in describing it in case they escape.

The workmen whom you see prowling the neighborhood may not be thieves per se, but they may be something almost as bad. Some small-time contractors make a practice of selling cut-rate (but almost worthless) home repair to householders unwary enough to fall for their scare stories of what might happen if the cesspool isn't drained or the driveway isn't repaved. By the time the unwary homeowner finds out that the asphalt they supposedly put on his driveway is nothing but a coat of cheap paint, or the siding they put up is substandard and overpriced, the wandering handymen have generally disappeared. If you see suspicious characters dressed as workingmen, they may be some of these wayfaring plunderers. So don't hesitate to call the police if you see something suspicious going on.

DELIVERY PEOPLE

Another favorite disguise of the thief is the guise of the delivery boy. Most delivery people are honest and hardworking, so they tend to build up a kind of public trust. This makes it easier for a thief to use this role for his own plans.

Any delivery person you haven't seen before should be watched closely. Don't accept delivery of anything you haven't ordered. Dropping off a package of some kind may be a ploy to get inside the house. If he tries to enter while you go back inside from the door to get your money, ask him politely to leave—and change the store you do business with. As a rule, it's a mistake to invite a delivery person into your house, not for any reasons of snobbery or class distinction, but because any stranger may turn out to be a thief or a thief's informant. Even if the delivery boy himself is too honest or too scared to try a break and entry by himself, he may tell his friends in school about some items of special interest or value inside your house and prompt an amateur burglary by high school kids. At some schools, in fact, a certain group of boys, or even of girls, may go in for petty crime for kicks and pocket money. These juvenile thrill-seekers can plunder your house just as effectively as a full-grown burglar, and probably make an even worse mess in the process. So, be careful when you think about letting a delivery boy inside your house. You may be opening the door to a Pandora's box of trouble with callow criminals not yet out of high school.

KIDS

Most burglaries are done by nonprofessionals. Some of these amateurs are drug addicts who have a desperate need for money, and others are people who, because of a lack of education, prejudice against them, or some other factor, are unable to get the kind of job they'd like or think they deserve.

But a surprising number of burglaries are pulled off by young people in their late teens or early twenties.

The teen years, for all the envy that older people may feel toward the young, are perhaps the worst years in a person's life, the only exception being extreme old age in poverty.

Today, because of improved nutrition, most children reach puberty, the threshold of biological maturity, in their early or mid-teens. Yet, because society requires that most people finish high school and preferably college, young people are denied their social and economic maturity until their early 20s. This leaves almost a decade of life in which the young person is in a sort of pampered prison: he may be an adult physically and may well be better informed, in fact, than his parents and the other adults who control his destiny, yet he is totally dependent on his parents and the adult world for support. Some parents, who themselves had to go to work at an early age in an era when education counted less than it does today, may aggravate the young person's sense of worthlessness by constantly railing about how easy kids today have it and how hard life was during the depression or the war. Other parents try to exert too much control over their children, forcing them to rebel to save their individuality. Still others, perhaps through selfishness or perhaps through sincere preoccupations with life outside the home, allow their children a totally free reign. All three types of parents, in effect, are recruiting officers for the vast underground army of juvenile vandals whose exploits sometimes shock and alarm the public in even the most affluent suburban communities.

Fortunately for the adult population of the world and America, not every teenaged kid is a hoodlum. The majority of young people accept their parents' values or limit their nonconformity to new styles of dress and speech and perhaps to some mild experimentation with soft drugs or liquor. The adolescent who can find an outlet in studies, in sports, or in romance is rarely a threat to society. But there are other youngsters, those who can't find any happiness in the school-room, on the gridiron, or even in the backseat. And these kids—born losers, as they sometimes call themselves with glum defiance—can raise hell with an ordered society that isn't equipped to cope with juvenile offenders.

The proverbial kids "with nothing to do" often turn their unresolved personality crises and endless spare time into full-scale attacks on the affluence around them. In one subur-ban town a few miles from New York City, with a high average income and quiet, treelined streets, high school up-perclassmen formed a club they called The Wreckers. The Wreckers would solicit from their friends and from unprinci-pled adults "shopping lists" of consumer goods that their clients wanted to buy "cheap." At certain parks or at taverns, an adult who wanted to buy a hi-fi or a color TV would link up with The Wreckers and give them the exact specifications. Within days, The Wreckers would break into private homes and steal everything on the list, to be sold to clients at a few pennies on the dollar.

Few, if any, of The Wreckers came from poor homes. Most had come from families that owned two or three cars and second homes in the mountains or at the shore. Their motiva-tions, besides petty cash to buy beer and marijuana, were thrills, defiance of the law, irritation at the dullness of the town they lived in, and a total contempt for the local police. Local police, in fact, knew who many of The Wreckers were, but lack of hard evidence, not to mention parental pressure from well-to-do families, kept the gang unscathed for several years. The Wreckers finally broke up when one key member was arrested on drug-pushing charges and two others were drafted.

In another town, a few miles from the first one, the juvenile underworld consisted of two rival gangs—Mission Ridicu-lous, named with an eye on the TV show *Mission Impossible*, and The Rebels, described by the other gang as punks who weren't tough enough to get into Mission Ridiculous. The two gangs waged a "shadow battle" to prove which was the bolder, and their competition surfaced every few weeks as the press reported some new outrage. At first, the pranks were fairly innocent. One gang somehow sent a partisan clambering up onto the roof of the municipal building, which housed the police station and firehouse, and the infiltrator pasted a large Mickey Mouse cutout onto the hands of the town clock.

A few weeks later, the other gang countered by sending their own second-story expert up the side of the building to tie a brassiere on the minute hand of the clock. How both groups escaped detection by the police is a subject for conjecture, and some embarrassment.

Competition grew more intense and damages increased. Each group painted their names on a town landmark with luminous paint, which meant two expensive sandblastings. Finally, all sense of fun vanished and the pranks became sheer malice. One night, vandals smashed their way into the town high school and did $2,000 worth of damage, breaking windows, smashing school science projects, and stealing tools and equipment from the machine shop and the science lab. This brought about a police crackdown, but no arrests were made—according to a rumor later privately confirmed by a disgusted detective, influential parents had dissuaded the police from making arrests because several of the suspects, fingered by informers, had already been admitted to prestigious colleges, including a military academy.

These situations took place not in a ghetto or a working town but in two of the richest suburbs in the New York area, in towns that were almost lily-white and college-oriented to the point that most of the younger breadwinners had graduate school credits. The parents of these Wreckers, Rebels, and Mission Ridiculous commandos weren't junkies, hookers, welfare mothers, and loafers, nor were they bitter immigrants living in poverty, or exploited coal miners; they were, for the most part, teachers, lawyers, dentists, small business owners, accountants, and skilled tradesmen—middle- and upper-middle-class consumers in a town famous for its excellent school system and its numerous parks and recreation areas.

The motley history of these upper-middle-class youth gangs should serve as a warning to anyone who thinks his property is safe from marauding teenagers just because he lives in an upper-income community far from city slums. Many middle-class or upper-income kids—nothing like a majority, but a surprisingly large number—break into homes just for the fun of it, with a chance to make some quick money as an incidental thrill.

Thus, when you leave your home or apartment, you should be on the lookout for the teenaged crowd. Most of them are not dangerous and wouldn't want to do you any physical harm. In fact, they might even come to your aid if your car broke down and needed a push. But this doesn't mean that they might not break into your apartment or house on a dare, or commit some other meaningless crime just to put on a show of bravado for their friends.

If you see a group of unruly teenagers wandering or congregating in your neighborhood, you should give the police a call. They will send a patrol car around to check on the teenagers and make sure that they don't get into trouble. Usually they will simply stop the car nearby and watch the youngsters for a while, or if the occasion warrants, send a patrolman over to talk to them.

Many adults, remembering when they were youngsters, will hesitate to call the police unless they see some real violence taking place. This attitude may be commendable, but it may not be wise. A large group of kids can get out of hand very quickly, especially if liquor or drugs is a factor; behavior that is merely unruly can become vicious on very short provocation. Young people have the same rights as other citizens in our society, but no extra rights. You wouldn't tolerate an adult or group of adults loitering around on street corners using filthy language or shouting innuendoes at passers-by, so you shouldn't tolerate this type of behavior from young people either.

Gangs of kids may limit their mischief to rude noises and heckling. On the other hand, if they get out of control, they may run completely amok, slashing tires, breaking car headlights, smashing windows in cars and homes, chopping down shrubbery, and even attacking grown-ups or other youngsters.

Whatever you do, don't attempt a direct confrontation with

the teenagers. If hot words lead to a fight, you could be liable to all kinds of legal troubles and vilification for punching a minor. On the other hand, a really bad kid, or just one who feels threatened, might do you serious injury. In some neighborhoods, almost any kid who walks the streets carries a weapon of some kind, usually for self-preservation. Even in middle-class or rich communities, almost everyone can cite at least one case of a boy (or girl) doing someone injury with a knife or gun.

Moreover, the kind of adult who makes a fetish of trying to be a surrogate father or Dutch Uncle to unruly kids often draws down their ire on himself. In the town where the Rebels and Mission Ridiculous were battling for fame or infamy, one elderly man made a habit of shouting at youngsters who walked across his property or otherwise violated what he thought were acceptable standards. They reciprocated by launching a full-scale attack on his house, pounding the door and shrieking curses at him and tearing up the flowers and shrubbery in his yard. Other adults have had cars run across their lawns, and in the town where the Wreckers held sway, a store owner who had charged several of the Wreckers and other delinquents, had his shop bombed. A pipe bomb blew up inside his building, shattering windows and nearly wounding a lodger's son with jagged fragments.

When dealing with obstreperous kids, even more than with adults, don't fall victim to the Wyatt Earp syndrome. Let the police do their job. They should thank you for it. When you call, simply inform the desk officer or dispatcher that there is a group of kids congregating near Jones Street. You don't even have to leave your name.

If you grew up in some less affluent town, you may feel a residual pang of guilt as a 'squealer' when you do this. Don't! You are really helping the teenagers as well as protecting your own property. Though they may hate the police harassment at the time, it may keep them from going on to commit serious illegal acts which could ruin their whole future. It's better for them to go through a little bit of adolescent *Weltschmerz* than to start breaking into houses for kicks and then keep it up until they get caught and start an adult criminal record. All criminals start small, many of them as teenagers. Perhaps by asking the police to break up a clique of noisy kids, you may keep some of them from progressing into serious trouble with the law.

IN PARKING LOTS

As we have said before, one crucial concern to the professional burglar or the serious amateur is finding out whether you're home or not. He has a lot of tricks, which we've already discussed, for doing just this. But he may also have access to another simpler trick. He may simply watch you leave home.

This is a special problem for people who leave their cars in parking lots, the kind attached to apartment houses and garden apartments. These lots are a great convenience, and you probably feel a lot more secure about leaving your car in its own marked space than you would about parking in the street. Unfortunately, you might just be dead wrong in this feeling.

If a thief's intended victim lives in an apartment house with attached parking, all he has to do is watch the lot and notice when the car leaves. If the thief knows what you look like and what kind of car you drive, this is the simplest thing in the world. And it's simpler yet if you have a reserved space with an apartment number or your name on it. The thief simply watches the parking place until the car is gone and then moves in. If the parking space is visible from the apartment, he can keep an eye on it and beat a quick retreat if the car drives back in. Thus having a reserved space may be a convenience, even a status symbol, but it also supplies the thief with notice as to whether you are at home or not, and even with a distant early warning system if he can see it.

How can you overcome this problem? First, you must be observant when entering and leaving the building. Take a close look around the area every time you go through the parking lot to see if there are suspicious characters loitering around.

Look at all the cars in the lot and see if someone is sitting in a car or, worse yet, hiding behind one. This, admittedly, would be pretty obvious for a professional crook, but if you see someone doing this, don't hesitate to report him to the supervisor.

A more competent crook may survey the parking lot from a distance, looking down from a nearby building or from an adjacent property. If you see someone who looks like he's keeping an eye on the lot, and then come back and see him still there an hour later, let the police know about it. It could be a false alarm—possibly even another policeman keeping the lot under surveillance looking for a suspect—but don't let that stop you. You could prevent a theft, a mugging, or perhaps something worse, by promptly reporting anyone loitering around the apartment.

8

Insurance

When all is said and done, there is no foolproof system to avoid being burglarized. The Egyptian pharaohs constructed all kinds of elaborate devices to protect their tombs and mummies, yet almost every royal tomb was robbed in ancient times. Some of the fabled jewels of Europe and Asia were stolen not once but several times. And modern security methods, as improved as they are by electronics, are unlikely to prevent a certain amount of burglary from being successfully carried out.

But modern man has one advantage over the pharaohs of Egypt or the potentates of Asia—he can insure his possessions so that, even if they are stolen, he can obtain their value back in cash and replace them, or at least buy reasonable facsimiles thereof.

Selecting the right insurance coverage is perhaps as important as selecting the right type of lock or the right home. The choice, however, is not quite as clear-cut. The homeowner who is interested in security should, of course, insist on a dead bolt lock and buy a home in a relatively crime-free neighborhood with proper lighting and regular police patrols, as we have discussed at length elsewhere. There is no similar single clear choice in purchasing insurance.

Most homeowners' policies provide some kind of protection against burglary, though this shouldn't be taken for granted. If you have a valid homeowner's policy, take it out and check it over to see how much theft coverage is provided. If there isn't any specific provision for theft protection, you should take out a theft protection policy or possibly change your homeowner's policy so that theft is covered.

Most of the available insurance policies are the same, although there are different wordings and various deductibles. But you can go to a major insurance company and expect to receive a certain quality of insurance coverage from all of them. The procedure is simple. You decide how much the valuables in your home are worth, and after reaching a total, go to the insurance agent and ask for coverage in this amount.

There are two different types of insurance agent, and the type you deal with makes a crucial difference to coverage. The first type of agent is an independent agent, and he will place your account with whatever insurance company you agree on with him. The other type of agent works for the insurance company itself, and in dealing with him or her, you are in effect dealing directly with the company.

The main difference in these two types of agents is the time it takes your policy to go into effect. If you deal with a private agent and he gets the insurance for you, you are not covered by the policy he obtains until the insurance carrier has sent word to you or to the agent that the policy exists.

For instance, if you go to the Joe Smith Insurance Agency and tell Joe you want $10,000 worth of theft insurance, Joe will take down the information about you, where you live, and what kind of policy you want. He will then contact several insurance companies on your behalf and arrange an insurance policy; you will pay Joe Smith, and he will pay the insurance company for the policy. He will ask you to sign some papers at his office or at your home or apartment, but you won't be covered until he finds the insurance carrier to accept the policy. This may take a week or so.

Let's say, however, that you go down to Joe's office, sign the papers, and pay him. On your return home, you discover that you've been burglarized. Once you're over the initial shock and outrage, you congratulate yourself on your foresight in getting insurance coverage. But your self-congratulations are premature. Until the carrier has accepted your policy from Joe Smith, you're not covered at all. Unless old Joe Smith wants to be a prince of a guy and step forward to pay for your losses out of his own pocket—figure the odds on that one as just about zero—you're stuck for the full losses of the theft.

If, however, you deal with an agent of the insurance company itself, rather than an independent agent, the situation is changed. As soon as you can sign the paper with the insurance agent, in most cases, you are covered by the policy immediately, before the ink is dry. This means that if you are burglarized on the way home, but you fulfill the policy's requirements, you will be covered for your losses up to the full amount of the policy.

Thus it's of more than passing importance to find out who the insurance agent works for before you sign. Find out whether he represents a specific firm or is an independent agent. This is the major difference. In both cases the fee would be the same. It stands to reason, however, that you should want to be protected as soon as possible, so if you deal with an independent agent, make sure that he has a carrier all lined up for you before signing.

The insurance policy will probably cover you for break and entry and for the value of objects stolen. This means that you are, first of all, covered for any damage the burglar does when he enters the house. This sort of damage can range from a broken window to a whole door ripped off. Obviously, break and entry alone can be expensive.

Some companies will require you to list everything of value inside your house or apartment to qualify for insurance coverage of these articles. Only the things you mention will be covered. If you state, for instance, that you want your TV, your jewelry, and your radio covered, the policy will cover this. If, in the meantime, you buy a stereo, but don't list it for coverage, the policy will not cover it. Make sure whether or not the policy you have requires a list of the items, and if it does, list everything of any value.

There are other companies which will protect anything in your house or apartment up to a certain price. They will not exceed this amount. Thus if you have a $10,000 policy and a thief breaks in and really cleans you out, taking valuables worth $20,000, you will be out $10,000. The insurance policy will only cover you for $10,000. So know how much it would cost to replace your possessions and have the policy state that amount. Do not, however, take out a policy for $50,000 if you only have $10,000 worth of possessions, in the hope of being able to collect $40,000 in gravy if you are ever plundered. It doesn't work that way. The company generally will only pay for the losses you have incurred, up to the full amount of your policy. It doesn't deal in windfalls for people lucky enough to be burglarized.

The legendary "fine print" in contracts, the subject of a good deal of laughter in comedies, is, in fact, quite important. You must be careful about the wording and carry out the requirements to the letter or your policy may be invalidated—which means that you get stung in case of a burglary.

The fine print may require you to do certain things, such as keeping photos of all your jewelry or using certain security devices. If the company can show that you didn't fulfill the requirements—no payment. If the policy states that you must keep the door locked when you leave the house and be the only person with a key to your apartment, and you leave the door open or give someone else a key, the policy will not cover you if anyone from the insurance company finds out. If a burglary occurs, you're on your own.

Insurance policies are basically similar, and most companies—though not all—are reputable. Check with friends and find out which companies in your area have the best reputation for paying off when burglaries or other mishaps occur, and pick the most reputable company. Read the fine print, and if you don't understand it, say so. After a burglary takes place, it will be too late to do anything but hope that you fulfilled the requirements and can collect.

REQUIREMENTS

In attempting to collect on an insurance policy, the requirements for collecting are of no small interest. This subject needs a look in depth before you contract for an insurance policy.

Most insurance companies are pleased to obtain you as a new account. They'll welcome you to their office, even serve coffee and cake and hope you sign on the dotted line. A few months after all this politeness and good fellowship, you may find yourself locked in a legal battle to prove certain things you didn't think about when you signed the contract. That's the nature of the game. Many people who would never dream of taking candy from a baby or holding up a service station wouldn't think twice about cheating an insurance company, and insurance fraud is a million-dollar-plus industry. Because of this, the insurance companies themselves may seem unnecessarily suspicious. They will often seem highly skeptical of even your most honest claims. This is because, quite simply, the insurance company and the customer are at odds: it is in your interest that the company pay; it is in their interest that they avoid paying.

There have been cases where a person purchased about $20,000 worth of insurance for a house from an independent agent. The insurance was a part of a homeowner's policy that included theft insurance. As most people would, the homeowner simply listened to the agent, signed up, took the policy home, and filed it away without reading the fine print.

But the insurance company, unknown to the customer, required that before a claim could be made and paid, the company had to have proof that the valuables had really existed and were in the owner's possession before they were stolen. The company also required the policyholder to report the crime to the police within twenty-four hours of discovery, and to notify the insurance company within forty-eight hours. There were other requirements as well, such as locking the door and keeping the windows closed, but these were not called into question.

When a thief broke into the house and stole $15,000 worth of property, the owner was quite naturally shocked. Yet he relaxed when he remembered that his insurance company covered the house for $20,000.

The owner called the police as soon as he discovered that he had been plundered. The following day, he called his insurance agent to report the theft. Unfortunately, the independent agent forgot to report the crime immediately, and it was two weeks before anyone at the agent's office remembered to report the theft to the insurance carrier. This was a violation of the original contract.

And it wasn't the only violation. The homeowner hadn't kept any receipts for the goods he owned and had never even made an inventory of his property. Thus he really didn't have proof that he owned the items he said he did. This was another violation of the contract requirements.

Not surprisingly, the insurance company gave the homeowner a hard time about paying for all the items that the owner claimed. He hadn't followed the rules that both of the parties had agreed upon through the contract. The homeowner, of course, wasn't aware that he was required to furnish proof or that he had technically failed to report the theft within the time limits, but ignorance of the law—or the contract—is no excuse. The insurance company paid for a TV set, a few radios, and other items which a person of the homeowner's income bracket would probably have owned, but refused to cover any special or unusual items because there was no acceptable proof that such items had ever existed. The company, to be fair, didn't even have to go as far as it did because the contract had been invalidated as soon as the homeowner failed to notify them of theft within forty-eight hours.

Ultimately, the insurance company paid the homeowner about $2,500 for the total $15,000 theft. Had the homeowner taken the time to read the fine print in his policy and conformed with the requirements, he probably would have recovered the total $15,000.

This case illustrates the pitfalls of overlooking fine print and depending excessively on the say-so of independent agents. You must know what you are signing and all the requirements. As long as the insurance company's requirements are fair and not unreasonable or of questionable legality, they will be upheld in court, and suing the company to regain losses they won't cover will be a waste of time.

INVENTORY

If the luckless homeowner in the story had kept a proper inventory, he could have collected a good deal more for his investment in insurance money. Thus a good inventory is vital for purposes of collecting insurance claims. It is also important in that it may help the police catch the thief or return some of your valuables.

In the event that your house is burglarized, the police will arrive at your call and ask for a list of the items stolen. Your responsibility is to provide the police with just such a list. The task may well be time-consuming and frustrating, to both you and the police, if this is the first time you've given it any thought. But if you have an inventory of your possessions prepared in advance, you can pick it up and walk from room to room, checking off the items that are missing. With such a list ready in advance, you can survey the damages in a few minutes to a half hour—hopefully, in time to help the police get some of your valuables back.

The easiest time to start an inventory is when you are just moving into the house. You can list the items, their descriptions, and the prices as they come into the house or are unpacked. This will be quick and efficient.

Unfortunately, most people don't move all that often and shouldn't wait until their next moving day, perhaps a decade in the future, to inventory their valuables. So they have to take some time from their normal schedule to do inventory.

Inventory in the retailing trade has overtones of total horror, though some stores try to make a party of it, with coffee and cake for employees and mandatory but profitable overtime. A home inventory needn't be this drastic. Set aside one full day for the process, and, if you can, get some help from family or very close friends.

Buy a folder of paper. On each page, separate the sheet into two columns. The first column is for the name of the object and perhaps a brief description: "mantel clock, with brass cupids"; "end table, scratch on leg," etc., etc. The second column is for the price. Give the exact purchase price if you have it. If not, look for a similar item in a catalogue and check the price. Try to keep the list up to date. Remember, some items—antique furniture, art objects—will probably appreciate with time, while others—appliances, electronic equipment—will probably depreciate. Nevertheless, since you'll be stuck with the task of replacing any goodies that are ripped off, put down what it would cost to get them back today.

Head the first page "Bedroom." Go through the bedroom and list every item over $50 that could be carted away by anyone smaller than King Kong. Include the smaller furniture and the lamps. If you have a TV or a clock radio in the bedroom, be sure to list that. And put a price with each item.

Continue this through the entire house. Head each new page with the name of the room and then list the item. You might even want to note the date that you are taking the inventory. Don't overlook any item of value that could be carted away. As a rule you should include any valuable furniture except perhaps the bed, refrigerator, and stove. There are probably some thieves who would steal the proverbial kitchen sink, but they'd have to go through the torments of hell disconnecting it, so you usually don't have to worry about that or the toilets. But list everything else. You never know when some enterprising band of rip-off men will disguise themselves as furniture movers and strip the cupboard totally bare. It has happened before.

The most likely bet is that you'll be astounded, and possibly gratified, to find out how much you own. Even lower-middle-class people today often own possessions that would make an eighteenth-century monarch green with envy. And the value of unexpected items can catch up on you. If your record collection is at all extensive, you could have thousands of dollars' worth of disks. Some may be valuable relics in themselves, but over and above their value on the market, the cost of replacing them all would be staggering. Books are another sleeper. A library of any size may be worth thousands, and some of the books may now be long out of print and impossible, or at least expensive, to replace. This is especially true if you have first-edition, nonfiction books.

After each room is completed—even assuming that you don't have extensive stocks of jewelry, rare books, fine old wine, or the world's largest collection of bottle caps—you will probably find that you own possessions worth well over $10,000. This may elate you and may shock you, but whatever it does for your self-image, it should indicate clearly how much insurance you need.

You should take out a policy to cover the total value of your property, both from theft and from fire. But unless you own the building, you should not take out more than the total worth of your movable possessions. To take out more insurance than you need would be a waste of money. If, for instance, you take out $20,000 worth of insurance to cover $10,000 worth of property, you'd be paying for twice as much insurance as you need, and you wouldn't be able to collect more than the worth of your stolen possessions in any case.

The only time when you should exceed the value of your actual possessions is when you are contemplating an additional purchase in the near future while contracting for the insurance. For example, if you have $15,000 worth of possessions but are contemplating the purchase of a $5,000 organ, it would be totally logical to take out a $20,000 policy.

After you have completed your inventory of present and expected purchases, you should make a copy of the list. One copy should be kept in the house or apartment and the other should be kept in a safety-deposit box in a bank. This is so that if the first list is destroyed in a fire—or perhaps stolen—the copy will be available to document the loss. As you make new purchases, you should update the home copy, and periodically update the safety-deposit-box copy, too. In this way, when it comes time to update your insurance, all you have to do is refer back to the inventory and see how much more insurance, if any, you need.

When you make new purchases, by all means keep the receipts. These will verify that you own (or owned) the items as well as confirm the purchase price. For items you may have owned for a long time and can't find the receipts for, you may want to have a friend take photographs of them. The photos need not be of Pulitzer Prize quality—a Polaroid Swinger or Kodak Instamatic will do the job. Should your ownership be questioned, this will at least give you a fighting edge in court.

But that shouldn't be necessary. If you can produce a dated inventory, the insurance company will probably accept your version of what possessions you actually owned and make restitution. One good way to have a binding date on any document is to take it before a notary public and have him note the date and affix his seal to it. This is relatively cheap—about 50 cents—and should save you a lot of grief if the matter ever comes up in court. Another method would be to mail yourself a copy of the list and keep it, unopened, in the postmarked and dated envelope. This is a method that authors use to protect their manuscripts from being co-opted, but it will work with any document that requires a definite date and some way of attesting to that date.

INSURANCE INVESTIGATION

When you have your inventory completed and your receipts or photographs assembled, you're ready for the acid test in dealing with an insurance company—the visit(s) from the *insurance claims investigator*.

Insurance claims investigators are a necessary part of the insurance business because, as we have said, insurance fraud is practically a national industry. People cheat insurance companies without remorse, and the insurance companies are in business to make money, not to give it away. So they employ people to investigate possible fraud in claims. At least one call from such an investigator is routine in any large-claim case.

Some investigators are really private detectives hired by the insurance company to protect its interests. These individuals may not look much like Mannix or Cannon, but they usually know their jobs and are often very tough, suspicious cookies. To get a private detective's license in most states you need at least five years of time on a recognized police force or the equivalent, besides passing tests of professional competence. Many investigators are career police officers who have retired, ex-FBI agents, and so forth. Others are people who took the jobs because nothing else was available but found they were good at it. In any case the investigators the company sends out are apt to be cynical and very thorough in their checking of claims.

Initially, the investigator will probably come to your house or apartment and just talk to you, probably asking the same questions that the police did. He'll also talk to the police. Depending on the amount of the claim, he will then report back as to whether he thinks there should be a further investigation. If the amount of the claim is reasonable and the evidence for a crime clear, this will probably be the last you'll see of him.

If the investigator thinks that there has been fraud and that the alleged crime is in fact a trick to get money from the insurance company under false pretenses, he'll continue the investigation. His first step will probably be to contact your friends and employer to find out if you or a member of your family has been in financial need. If he learns that you have been, his suspicions will probably increase. Most middle-class people who turn to insurance fraud and other white-collar crimes are propelled into breaking the law because they can't earn enough at their regular jobs to meet unforeseen expenses, which may range from a loved one's operation to gambling debts, girl friends, or compulsive spending on luxuries.

Having established your need for quick cash, the investigator will watch you and your family to see if any of the articles supposedly stolen turn up in your possession. He may also keep an eye on your bank accounts to see if you've made any major deposits that haven't been used for home repair and replacing stolen goods. This checkup may take a day or two if the claim filed is small and the suspicion slight. But it could go on for months, or even years, if the claim is a really big one.

If the investigator can prove that the policyholder is faking and that no burglary in fact took place, the company can charge you with insurance fraud and have you arrested. People do go to jail for insurance fraud.

Most cases, however, are legitimate and are not investigated to any great degree. Unless your claim is really large—say between $20,000 and $50,000—your chances of having an insurance investigator really probe your life and finances are almost nil. It just wouldn't be worth the trouble for the company to put a man on the case every time somebody claims $500 or $1,000.

Investigators are a necessary evil. Without their services, insurance fraud would be far more common than it is, and insurance costs would skyrocket. The casual insurance chiseler may think he's getting back at Big Business when he files a bogus claim, but the real victims are the policyholders, who have their rates jacked up as the company pays out more in claims. If and when you do file a claim and the insurance investigator shows up, don't take it as a personal affront and begin to make indignant threats of suit for defamation of character. Sending an investigator out to check each claim, at least once, is a matter of form, and if you've lived up to your part of the insurance contract, you have nothing to fear.

THE COST

Having discussed what theft insurance is supposed to do, it's only natural to discuss what it costs. Most insurance policies are roughly the same in terms of regulations and protection, but they differ widely as to price from area to area, even from town to town. Buying insurance policies isn't as easy as comparison shopping from one supermarket to the other in quest of a bag of carrots which may cost 19 cents at one store and 49 cents at another and be relatively similar. The prices of insurance policies are based, quite logically, on several consistent factors.

The initial factor is where the policy owner lives—the town and its crime rate. Even if you don't know what the crime rate in your home town is, you can be sure that the insurance companies will. They take great pride in keeping accurate statistical tabs on every aspect of human life, most assuredly including the crime rate, so that they can compute their rates to provide coverage and make a profit at the same time.

If, for example, you live in a town with a relatively low crime rate, you may pay as little as $30 a year for theft insurance on a four-room apartment. To cover a house in the same area for break and entry and theft loss may cost about $100. If, however, you live in a town or section of the state with a high crime rate, you may pay $500 to insure an apartment and $1,000 to protect a house. This is, quite obviously, because you stand a much greater statistical chance of being robbed, and the company wants to make a profit from your policy.

Prices, of course, also vary according to the amount of coverage you want. The price will usually rise in direct relation to the amount of coverage you want. In other words, if you get coverage with a ceiling of $10,000 for $30 a year, it would cost you $60 a year to raise the ceiling to $60,000.

Occurrences are also a factor. The number of times a house has been entered and claims have been made against the company will affect the cost of a policy on that particular house. The same is true of auto insurance. People who have a lot of automobile accidents have to pay more for insurance than those drivers whose records are clean. People whose houses are burglarized have to pay more for insurance the next time around. A sense of fairness is lacking here, of course, since it's usually easier to prevent an automobile accident than it is to prevent a burglary. But the insurance company is in business to make money, and statistics are all they have to go on.

Take the case of a family which has lived in the same house for the past ten years. For the first five, they had no burglaries and the rates for insurance were low. But the crime rate increased, and their house was broken into five times in the last two years. Thus their insurance rate soars because they have become, statistically, victimized at a greater rate than their neighbors, and predictably they will continue to be burglarized at about an average rate.

This is how insurance is priced. Yet despite the fact that most companies employ the same criteria for setting prices, there may be a considerable difference in the prices of similar policies. When you have decided exactly what kind of coverage you want, go to several different companies and see what prices they quote. Make sure that you take down full details on what kind of coverage they're offering for the price. Don't rush into any agreement. Use the prices cited, the coverage promised, and the company's reputation to decide which brand of insurance you want to buy.

Don't be snowed into buying from any particular company by massive TV or radio ad campaigns. Though most larger companies spend substantial sums of money on TV time and other sources of publicity, a heavy ad campaign doesn't prove anything about a company. One independent broker, who ran a huge late-night TV campaign, in which he appeared in person and urged young drivers or those with faulty records to come in and get covered at bargain prices, went bankrupt while his ads were still playing on TV and left hundreds of drivers with no coverage at all. He had been accepting the premiums but had neglected to forward them on to carriers. This created a fantastic mess for the people who signed up with him.

When buying insurance, let the company's prior record, rather than sales pitches, be your best guide as to what to expect. If you deal with an independent broker, make certain just how long he expects to take to lodge your policy with a carrier and see that he sticks to this timetable.

Perhaps the best antitheft insurance is the part that comes with a standard homeowner's policy that protects the householder against such liabilities as people suing when they trip on his steps, storm damage, and fire. Theft insurance tucked into this package is apt to be painless and economical, and for a yearly sum of $30 to $60 for an apartment or $100 for a home, you and your possessions can be protected from burglary. In terms of piece of mind alone, the feeling of protection should be worth the money.

CONCLUSION

When you first picked up this book, you were wondering if there was any foolproof way to protect yourself against burglary. As you can surmise from reading the book, there is, in fact, no totally foolproof protection. But there are enough kinds of partial protection to make the crucial difference when your house or apartment is the tentative target of a prowler.

Granted, a team of highly skilled burglars, the kind that steal jewels from museums or documents from foreign embassies, can probably penetrate any screen you can throw around your home at a reasonable price. Tales of espionage are full of the accounts of spies and saboteurs who bypassed complex protection systems to break into safes and steal code books or microfilm, or of bold thieves who stole priceless gems from closely guarded vaults and museums. So why even try to set up a security system that can't guarantee absolute safety?

The answer should be fairly obvious if you've been reading closely. Most burglars aren't skilled jewel thieves or spies. Most of them are fairly casual criminals who will bypass a really tough job in favor of something easy.

Think about this: There is no such thing as a bulletproof steel helmet. Any helmet made can be pierced by a high-powered rifle bullet or machine-gun slug, let alone a direct shell hit. But every European army continues to issue steel helmets by the million to its soldiers, for two reasons. The first is that the helmet can stop a large variety of projectiles—spent rifle bullets, pistol slugs, shell fragments that aren't direct hits, flying rocks, and other potentially lethal flying metal that might otherwise kill the soldier wearing the helmet. These objects, in modern combat, cause more battlefield deaths than direct hits from rifle fire. Thus the helmets literally save thousands of lives, even though they can't save everybody. The second reason is psychological. A soldier who wears a helmet feels increased self-confidence, and is usually braver than one who wears a cap. He may be less afraid of shellfire. Thus he is better able to accomplish his mission.

The same is true of home safety. You may never be able to afford or install a security system that will stop a serious attempt at forcible entry by skilled professional burglars—a direct hit, in other words, by a high-powered rifle. But any intelligent system you devise will greatly decrease the odds of a break-in by kids, by clumsy amateurs, or even by the less adept professional thieves—the glancing hits, so to speak. Since most burglaries are not long-term-planning premeditated jobs but glancing hits on a quick sweep through a town or neighborhood, the security system within your reach may be good enough to save you a lot of grief.

High-class security, the kind that you need if you own a mansion full of art and jewels, is a different game from the simple protection of a middle-class home whose most valuable possession may be a color TV or a stereo set. It's rather like the armored warfare race that existed during World War II. Both sides began the war with relatively thin-armored tanks and antitank guns of about 37 millimeters. It soon developed that the antitank guns couldn't always penetrate the armor even of existing tanks, so a crash program began to convert heavier antiaircraft guns to antitank use. At the same time, both sides began to rush heavier-armored tanks into production to cope with the new antitank guns. This trend continued all through the war, to such a degree that by mid-war the Germans and Russians were building tanks so big and heavy that they couldn't be shipped on standard flatcars and had to ford rivers with airtight hulls and breather tubes; they would have collapsed most bridges. In 1939, a respectable tank had a 37 millimeter gun and about a half inch of frontal armor. By war's end in 1945, a heavy tank would carry a gun of anywhere from 88 to 122 millimeters and have 4 to 5 inches of frontal armor.

There is an analogy between tank production and really intense security techniques. Each move is met by a countermove. The best that the museum proprietors and mansion owners can really hope for is to keep one jump ahead of the high-class crooks who plot the plunder of high-priced goodies. There will probably never be a foolproof burglar deterrent, even for those who can afford sky-high prices. Of course, you can hire a whole army to protect your possessions and that may be relatively foolproof. No one has broken into Fort Knox recently and looted the nation's gold reserve. You can cast your most treasured possessions inside a block of carbon steel, and thieves won't be able to get at them. But, of course, neither will you. A certain insecurity is part of owning priceless possessions.

If this book can't guarantee you total security, it can at least help you to know your enemy and to take appropriate measures to frustrate his devious designs. Having read this book, you should have a firm knowledge of how burglars operate.

To summarize: The day burglar uses the telephone, notes on bulletin boards, and gossip to find out which homes will be empty during the day. He may also check empty parking places or keep your house under surveillance if he's seriously interested.

The night burglar simply cruises around looking for poorly lit houses or apartments or those with other signs of vacancy to break into. Relevant chapters contain thorough information on how to convince the casual observer that you are home even when you're long gone.

Burglars don't wear raccoonlike masks or walk around with stubble on their chins and guns bulging from their pockets. The only way to spot a thief is by his actions. This also has been covered extensively. You have also been encouraged, repeatedly, to call the police if you see or seriously suspect anything suspicious. This is your best defense.

Where should you live to avoid being burglarized? You have full information on how to use federal statistics, local clerk's records, and a little deductive reasoning and mathematics to find out which towns are relatively crime-free.

How can you make your otherwise attractive home repellent to burglars? This has been thoroughly covered, with an eye toward helping you do some needed landscaping at minimal costs.

What security devices are the best for your purposes? The standard devices available have all been described with a look at their strengths and weaknesses and a concern for what will best suit your needs and budget. Beyond the very strong admonition to insist on a dead bolt lock on every outer door and to demand adequate lighting, the choices have been left up to you.

Should you buy a dog? Probably. Should you buy a gun?

Probably not. But the pros and cons of each decision have been discussed at length here and the choice remains yours.

There is a greater choice, the greatest choice of all. This is the choice between action and inaction. The war against crime may seem absolutely hopeless as statistics mount year by year, and with apathy a national problem, it is predictable that a majority of people—perhaps even you—will simply shrug and conclude that the situation is hopeless and decide to do nothing and take their chances. It's a free country—though manifestly not a crime-free one—and if you want to take this attitude, no one can stop you. No one can force you to protect your home from intruders. It *is* possible to paint lurid pictures of the consequences of a break and entry that may be more serious than a simple burglary, such as an attack by murderers or sexual perverts which could destroy your life or your children's. And even in an ordinary nonviolent burglary, the victims often report a sense of violation of their privacy that upsets and troubles them for months. Last but not least, of course, is the certainty, if you are burglarized, of losing expensive and perhaps sentimental objects which may be costly or impossible to replace. What price would you put on your engagement ring? Or on your grandmother's one silver coffee urn that she bought when she was just married? Or the jewels from the Old Country, whatever it may be? How about that painting you and your wife or husband bought to furnish your first apartment, when you felt it was extravagant but had to do it anyway?

Items like these are hard to replace, in your house or in your heart.

Obviously, the shock of having your home ripped apart and losing valuable and treasured possessions is a considerable blow to your equilibrium. Compare it to an automobile accident, which is probably more familiar to most people. The first shock is the collision: the noise, the fear, the chance of physical injury or death. After that come the liabilities: Did you kill or injure someone who may sue you? Will you have to bear the guilt of a person's death for the rest of your life? Then come the financial troubles: How much will this cost? Will your insurance go up? Could you lose your driver's license?

Then there is the recrimination: How could you be so stupid as to let this happen? You blame yourself for the damage to both cars and the rude intrusion into somebody else's life, even if no one was hurt. Lastly, there is the sheer physical inconvenience. While your car is in the shop, you'll have to hunt around for another one or use public transportation. If you live in the suburbs, you know what a pain in the neck this will be.

Just the same reactions set in after a burglary. The chance of death or injury, or of liability, is always there. If you break in and the burglar is still there, he may panic and kill you. Hard as life often is, few people really want to die in the middle of it. Death is the ultimate inconvenience.

But suppose you fly into a rage and somehow kill or injure the burglar. Ridiculous as it seems, we have shown that you could be hauled into court on assault or homicide charges and actually wind up spending time in jail.

Then there is the remorse. The same kind of person who never did anything to deter a burglar may very well begin to blame himself if a burglary did take place. Insurance costs? Your homeowner's policy is bound to climb every time you are burglarized. Inconvenience? You may wind up going without a TV or stereo for weeks or months after you are robbed. Other valuables such as original art or rare jewelry may never be replaced. Every time you look at the place where some cherished object stood on display, you may feel a pang of remorse.

Make no mistake about it, being burglarized is just as bad as being involved in an automobile accident, maybe a good deal worse. Yet if you drive a car, you have no choice but to accept the possibility that someday you may have an accident. If you live in a house or an apartment or anywhere else except a pallet on Skid Row, you have to accept the possibility that you may be burglarized.

You also have to take action to prevent it. No sane person would dream of driving around with his eyes closed, or of driving a car with faulty brakes or no lights. Yet the same motorist who would insist on perfect visibility, on good brakes and working headlights might never think of trimming the shrubbery around his front door to give the police a chance for surveillance of his front door, or of installing a dead bolt lock and front and side lighting to protect his home, which is a lot more expensive than his car. Hopefully, this book will jar a good many such people out of their apathy.

Apathy is, perhaps, the real secret enemy in the war against crime. Because of social apathy, neighborhoods turn into slums and apartments into tenements, where crime seems to many a normal occupation and a way of striking back at the outside world. Because of parental apathy, bored kids turn into thrill-seeking delinquents and contribute to the groundswell of petty crime and malicious mischief. Because of political apathy, the court system remains a battlefield for aggressive lawyers, where guilt or innocence matters less than the relative skill of the prosecution and defense attorneys. Because of official apathy, prisons remain factories for crime, where mixed-up kids are processed into hardened and sophisticated criminals.

Apathy also prevents a good many homeowners from doing anything about protecting their own property. Apathy has become fashionable, even sophisticated, in some circles. "When the rape is inevitable, relax and enjoy it," one cynical college maxim runs. And some people still give lip service to the hoary cliché, "You can't fight City Hall," even though the last ten years have marked the struggle of minorities, students, and women who fought City Hall and won.

Let the apathy stop with you. Corny as it may sound, it is clearly in your interest to turn your house into a fortress in the war against crime. Don't be satisfied just to know about watchdogs, sensors, silent alarms, dead bolt locks, and adequate lighting. Do something about them. Go to your phone book now and see how many locksmiths and security system planners there are in your immediate area. Tonight or tomorrow, ask your friends what they are doing to protect their houses or apartments from break and entry.

The day after tomorrow may be too late.

Index